Jane

May T

Keep you

M. Matranga

8/9/18

# Dreams

## A LANGUAGE OF
## The Holy Spirit

MAUREEN MATARANYIKA

authorHOUSE®

*AuthorHouse™ UK*
*1663 Liberty Drive*
*Bloomington, IN 47403  USA*
*www.authorhouse.co.uk*
*Phone: 0800.197.4150*

*Scripture quotations marked NKJV are taken from the New King James Version. Copyright © 1982 by Thomas Nelson, Inc. Used by permission. All rights reserved.*

*Scripture quotations marked NIV are taken from the Holy Bible, New International Version®. NIV®. Copyright © 1973, 1978, 1984 by International Bible Society. Used by permission of Zondervan. All rights reserved. [Biblica]*

*Published by AuthorHouse  06/19/2018*

*ISBN: 978-1-5462-9399-6 (sc)*
*ISBN: 978-1-5462-9398-9 (e)*

*Print information available on the last page.*

# Dedication

My short dedication is to my lovely daughter Anita Lamb, whom God has taught a lot through visions and dreams. To my son Timothy Tinodiwa and my daughter Pamela Musunga and my son Robert Lamb. To my daughters Mercy and Maud and the entire Ignite Global Prayer Ministries Church in Sittingbourne. Thank you to my church leadership, Sibongile Thabane, Pamela Musunga, and Robert Lamb.

I would also like to thank a few friends who have been of great encouragement who have walked with me and supported me: Noline Chikwaka, Dr Harriet Sziao, Rebbecca Zorph, Ivy Chiwandire, and Rita Phiri. To my mentors, Bill and Janet Findlatter, Urania, Ken Lukehurst, Robin Jegede Brimson, and my encouragers, Chipo Mudere, Angie Ndlalambi, and Silas Nyadzo. And to some very special people, my grandchildren, Josiah Lamb, Anna Lamb, and Maud Phiri.

For God speaks again and again, though people do not recognize it. He speaks in dreams and visions of the night when deep sleep falls on people as they lie in their beds. He whispers in their ears. (Job 33 vs 14–16 NKJV)

# The Purpose of this Book

God wants to give us many assurances of His readiness to bless, to heal, and to speak the many things He wants to do in the future. He also gives us conditions. One of them is to align us with His will and His word and walk in obedience. We are warned, taught, and instructed towards holy living. Dreams are not meant to arouse curiosity and promote guesswork for grace and truth came by Jesus Christ, He revealed the Rhema and the Logos, so there is no need for us to rely on superstition about God, but His word and His revelation. Jesus Christ made prophetic statements in Matthew 24, predicting what would take place before He returned. God uses dreams to remind us to pay attention to God's word. Knowing God's plans with us undergirds our confidence in His sovereignty and omniscience—He is in control, and He knows the end from the beginning.

# Preface

It's not a good idea to keep a dictionary of dreams to get the meanings of specific dreams. Because we receive dreams from the Lord, common themes, objects, animals, and colours can mean different things to different people, based on their associations, culture, and experiences.

My prayer is that every individual will develop His or Her own dream language by discerning the meaning of recurring symbols in their dreams. For example, I come from a background where people are buried in the ground after death and have never experienced cremations. Whenever there's going to be a death in my family, I always dream of people preparing the ground to plant a seed. After a long time of observing this warning, I realised it meant someone close to me was going to be laid to rest.

Having said that, there are some common symbols in the body of Christ that may hold the same meaning despite traditional and cultural beliefs.

God speaks again and again, although people do not recognise it. He speaks in dreams and visions of the night when deep sleep falls on people as they lie in their beds. He whispers in their ears.

# Introduction

Carl Yung wrote this about dreams: "A dream is like a theatre in which the dreamer himself is on the scene, the player, the prompter, the producer, the author, and the critic."

Should we attach any importance to our dreams? Can we teach ourselves to dream? We dream almost every night, but we often fail to grasp the importance of the message being uploaded to us from the spiritual realm.

Dreams carry personal messages to us and offer us opportunities to understand our lives better to archive greater inner harmony. Dreams help us to solve practical personal problems and help show us a way forward in times of trials and persecutions. We should seek to understand dreams and ask the Lord for the meaning of each dream, aligning them to the word of God so we can get the interpretation that relates to the spiritual food we digest.

Dreams are a huge part of our mental and social life. When we find that we can't interpret them, we need to ask God, and other people who may be gifted in the same area, for revelation. Remember, it's very important to seek answers from people who have a deep relationship with God. Pharaoh found Joseph, who had a relationship with God, and Nebuchadnezzar found Daniel to interpret His dreams. But you can go to just anyone; the devil will take advantage of people who do not know where to go for interpretation.

All of humanity knows that we dream—the great and small, the poor and the rich, black and white, educated and non-educated. On the intrinsic aspect of all dreams, thousands of years ago, men believed that by seeking their interpretation, they could solve all their problems. Psychologists and great philosophers all agree on the ability to dream, but in this book, I hope to give you some biblical input on this channel of communication between God and his people. My evidence is going to be based on the revealed word of God.

Dreaming involves the brain and the body. Sometimes when one is dreaming, there is an increase in heart rate and breathing. Some people scream and shout. Some show signs of physical movement, as if engaged in a fight or running. Many scientists suggest that dreams are just memories from long ago being played in the subconscious, yet trying to understand dreams will bring direction to the dreamer.

## Chapter 1

# WHAT THE BOOK OF JOB
# SAYS ABOUT DREAMS

The book of Job is one of the oldest books in the Bible. This book centres on human suffering, but its conclusion is the sovereign intervention of God. Job describes Himself as a man who tried to live an upright life, even becoming a priest and an intercessor for his family, yet bad things happened to Him. Job sought answers as to why he suffered but never seemed to understand why. Today, because we read the whole Bible, we understand that Job suffered because Satan accused Him of selfless devotion to God. In the story of Job, sin and suffering were connected. In summary, this book teaches us that righteous people suffer. We also learn that Satan cannot harm God, but He can attack a man who loves God and influence Him to walk away from God. He tries to make men attack God. Job defends the character of God.

Today, we can learn a lot from this book of job. We are living in the end times, and the devil has managed to turn many people away from God. He speaks to men with demonic questions like the following:

- If God is a loving father, why do children die?
- Why are people dying of cancer?
- Why are there wars?
- Why is there so much evil?
- Why are people hungry?
- Why is He silent when we pray?
- Does He speak to anyone?

These are only a few, but there are many other such demonic questions. In his suffering, Job utters a profound prophetic word. "I know my Redeemer lives and that in the end, He will stand on earth" (Job 19:25). Here He is pointing out that He knew God in the present. He was acquainted or had experienced His presence because He had revealed Himself to Job. He had given Job an understanding and knowledge of Him. Somewhere in the past, Job must have had an encounter with the Redeemer. The answer to all this comes from a few verses of Job (33:14–18):

> "For God may speak in one way, or in another,
> *Yet man* does not perceive it.
> [15] In a dream, in a vision of the night,
> When deep sleep falls upon men,
> While slumbering on their beds,
> [16] Then He opens the ears of men,
> And seals their instruction.
> [17] In order to turn man *from his* deed,
> And conceal pride from man,
> [18] He keeps back his soul from the Pit,
> And his life from [c]perishing by the sword."

God speaks in dreams, yet man does not regard the voice. He does not understand it. He is not aware that dreams are the voice of God, nor does He receive the things that are revealed for they are foolishness to him. He stops his ears and stands by his own choice. Yet God wants to keep him from sin and save Him them from hell. A long time back, Job figured this out and announced his conviction that God speaks. He is not silent, but people refuse to take note of His voice. It's clear from the writing in the book that Job was not moved by the trials because He was clear about whom He served and had a personal relationship with Him.

We are approaching a prophetic era where the scriptures will soon be fulfilled. Joel 2:28 is the primary source Acts 2:17 says, "And it shall come to pass afterward, that I will pour out my spirit on all people. Your sons and daughters will prophesy, your young men will see visions, your old men will dream dreams." The end time revival is marked by prophetic and apostolic anointing. Job saw this day in the spirit. There was clarity on His utterance that the redeemer—Christ would appear in physical form on earth. Jesus Christ promised the pouring out of the Holy Spirit. We are now in that day. It is very easy for people to identify the other gifts of prophecy and apostolic work, but the same group of people will decide to ignore the work of the Holy Spirit in dreaming prophetic dreams and visions. Dreams call us to change so we will not perish.

## Chapter 2

# ABRAHAM

In the Old Testament, we learn of several people whom God revealed Himself to in dreams. Dreams have been common since time immemorial, and even today, they play a great part of our lives. In this writing, names are mentioned of people whom God visited and whose lives He directed. We read in Genesis of the call of Abraham, and when we get to chapter 15, verse 1, we see God using a vision to restate His covenant:

> "After these things the word of the Lord came to Abram in a vision, saying, "Do not be afraid, Abram. I *am* your shield, [a]your exceedingly great reward."
>
> 2 But Abram said, "Lord God, what will You give me, seeing I [b]go childless, and the heir of my house *is* Eliezer of Damascus?" 3 Then Abram said, "Look, You have given me no offspring; indeed one[c] born in my house is my heir!"
>
> 4 And behold, the word of the Lord *came* to him, saying, "This one shall not be your heir, but one

4

who will come from your own body shall be your heir." ⁵ Then He brought him outside and said, "Look now toward heaven, and count the stars if you are able to number them." And He said to him, "So shall your descendants be."

⁶ And he believed in the Lord, and He accounted it to him for righteousness.

⁷ Then He said to him, "I *am* the Lord, who brought you out of Ur of the Chaldeans, to give you this land to inherit it."

These things were happening in a vision.
In Genesis 15:12-13:-

"Now when the sun was going down, a deep sleep fell upon Abram; and behold, horror *and* great darkness fell upon him. ¹³ Then He said to Abram: "Know certainly that your descendants will be strangers in a land *that is* not theirs, and will serve them, and they will afflict them four hundred years."

When Abraham was in a deep sleep, God painted an eternal picture to show to him. His natural children, those that shall be like the sand, would multiply and be tormented in Egypt. The tormentors (Egyptians) would trample upon them and oppress them in a wicked manner. He promised a great deliverance through Moses and their final journey to the land of Canaan. The second interpretation of this vision, however, talks of His spiritual children as being as numerous as the stars. The heirs of Heaven, strangers and pilgrims on this earth shall suffer persecution (John 15:18-19). Those that are blessed and beloved of God are often solely afflicted, by wicked men and systems—these are driven to the courts and persecuted but hold onto the deliverer. Jesus Christ has already paid the price for that journey to the heavenly Canaan. This family of Abraham was a seed born on Calvary, called from many nations. God's covenant with Abraham is about to be fulfilled—and very soon.

In dreams and visions, we see symbols. The smoking furnace and the burning lamp in Genesis 15:17–21 probably represents the Israelites' severe trials and joyful deliverance. This furnace and lamp, as they were passed between the pieces, burnt and consumed them and so completed the sacrifice and testified to God's acceptance of it (Jeremiah 34:18-20) (Exodus 18:19). Therefore, it's intimated that God's covenants with men are made with sacrifice.

In dreams, we learn that God addreses spiritual matters through natural situations. Abram was looking for a natural heir, but God was planning the salvation of all mankind. The promises He was making had a long view in focus; with the passing generations, the descendants of Abraham and Sarah would number in the millions. It is righteousness when we believe God and take Him at His word. God made Abraham sleep, so he contributes nothing to the covenant, and for us, we do nothing, contributing nothing for our salvation. Jesus Christ took upon Himself the curse that was meant for us, and He hung on a tree. God lives up to His promise, providing the sinless Lamb to take away the sin of the world. When we meet one day in heaven, we will rejoice with the natural family of Abraham that (are)I like the sand of the seashore and the spiritual family, those that are like the stars of Heaven. Even Abraham and Sarah will understand the meaning of that dream when we are all gathered beyond the river of life. Hallelujah!

*Chapter 3*

# JACOB'S LADDER

When we were young we loved to sing the song:

*We are climbing Jacob's ladder*
*We are climbing Jacob's ladder*
*X2*
*Soldier of the cross*

*Sinner, do you love my Jesus*
*Sinner, do you love my Jesus*

*X2*
*Soldier of the cross*

This song meant nothing to me until in my later years, when I realised that Jacob's Ladder was an experience he had in a dream. So profound was his dream that it outlived him, as do many dreams of eternal significance. The story of this dream is related in Genesis 28:10–22.

"Now Jacob went out from Beersheba and went toward Haran. [11] So he came to a certain place and stayed there all night, because the sun had set. And he took one of the stones of that place and put it at his head, and he lay down in that place to sleep. [12] Then he dreamed, and behold, a ladder *was* set up on the earth, and its top reached to heaven; and there the angels of God were ascending and descending on it.

[13] And behold, the Lord stood above it and said: "I *am* the Lord God of Abraham your father and the God of Isaac; the land on which you lie I will give to you and your descendants. [14] Also your descendants shall be as the dust of the earth; you shall spread abroad to the west and the east, to the north and the south; and in you and in your seed all the families of the earth shall be blessed. [15] Behold, I *am* with you and will keep[c] you wherever you go, and will bring you back to this land; for I will not leave you until I have done what I have spoken to you."

[16] Then Jacob awoke from his sleep and said, "Surely the Lord is in this place, and I did not know *it*." [17] And he was afraid and said, "How awesome *is* this place! This *is* none other than the house of God, and this *is* the gate of heaven!" [18] Then Jacob rose early in the morning, and took the stone that he had put at his head, set it up as a pillar, and poured oil on top of it. [19] And he called the name of that place [d]Bethel; but the name of that city had been Luz previously. [20] Then Jacob made a

vow, saying, "If God will be with me, and keep me in this way that I am going, and give me bread to eat and clothing to put on, [21] so that I come back to my father's house in peace, then the Lord shall be my God. [22] And this stone which I have set as a pillar shall be God's house, and of all that You give me I will surely give a [g]tenth to You."

When we look at the stream in the natural, we see that God holds the affairs of men both in heaven and on earth. The ladder reaches heaven, yet His dealings were with a mere man on the run. There was activity on this ladder— angels going up and some coming down, constant intercourse between heaven and earth. We see this every day in our lives—new babies delivered, something of heaven coming to the earth each day and souls departing from earth being received into heaven.

Spiritually we can accept that Christ, the son of the living God, is ladder, the foot on earth, His human nature, the top in heaven in His divine nature. Christ is the way all God's favours come to us and all our services go to Him. Our worship, our prayers, our giving all go to him, and His blessing, presence, (His)his healing, all come down to us. It's a two-way relationship. When our praises go up, His glory comes down.

Isaac blessed Jacob before he set out on his journey. It's important for all of us in our journey of life to get parental blessing before we cry out for God's blessing. Isaac received his blessing from his own father before the time came to pass it on (Genesis 17:19–21). The day after receiving is blessing, Jacob travelled forward, anxious and oppressed, fearing as he went farther away from his home - feelings of guilt over the stealing of the birthright blessing; however, yearned to hear God for himself to affirm that blessing. His mind was on the blessing as he wondered how to maintain such a stolen gift. He looked for divine affirmation and then laid himself to sleep, but his mind desired the divine interaction. He saw a ladder, and it told him heaven and earth are united. The things happening here on earth are orchestrated by God. Jacob saw right before him messengers of God ascending and descending on a staircase. At the head of the staircase, God Himself stood Genesis 24:13. God Himself confirms to Jacob in that dream all the promises made to Abraham and assures him of His constant presence and protection. The councils of God are executed on earth, and the affairs of this earth are well-known in heaven. There's nothing that mankind has that is not recorded in heaven. Everything small and great is handled with intricate precision and recorded in the books of heaven. Angels are employed as ministering spirits to serve all men, and the wisdom of God is at the upper end of the ladder, directing all motions of second causes of His glory. Angels ascend and descend, giving precise information, all the ins and outs of our daily activities. The dream was not meant to scare Jacob but to reassure and comfort him.

Today that ladder represents Christ, the mediator between God the Father and mankind. We can't go to the Father except through Jesus Christ, our Lord. The foot of earth is His human nature; the top is His divine nature, or we can say the earth stands for his humiliation on the cross, and the top His is eternal exaltation. Christ is the way all God's favours come to us. Jacob was to have a part in providing a physical lineage for the Messiah, but God was ultimately in control of bringing those promises to pass. God, when speaking to Jacob in Genesis 28:13-14 said, "I am the Lord God of your father Abraham." He did not say "grandfather". In covenant, we are all sons of God through Abraham. God promised him land and seed and the blessing in that seed for all of humanity. God was not just talking about natural things to Jacob but of the kingdom established through Christ. So we can see the language of the Holy Spirit that this was.

*Chapter 4*

# JOSEPH'S DREAM

By now we have established some of the dreamers. Next up in the genealogy is none other than one of the well-projected dreamers of all times: Joseph. The story includes Genesis 37:2–36.

"This *is* the history of Jacob.

Joseph, *being* seventeen years old, was feeding the flock with his brothers. And the lad *was* with the sons of Bilhah and the sons of Zilpah, his father's wives; and Joseph brought a bad report of them to his father.

³ Now Israel loved Joseph more than all his children, because he *was* the son of his old age. Also he made him a tunic of *many* colors. ⁴ But when his brothers saw that their father loved him more than all his brothers, they hated him and could not speak peaceably to him.

⁵ Now Joseph had a dream, and he told *it* to his brothers; and they hated him even more. ⁶ So he said to them, "Please hear this dream which I have

dreamed: [7] There we were, binding sheaves in the field. Then behold, my sheaf arose and also stood upright; and indeed your sheaves stood all around and bowed down to my sheaf."

[8] And his brothers said to him, "Shall you indeed reign over us? Or shall you indeed have dominion over us?" So they hated him even more for his dreams and for his words.

[9] Then he dreamed still another dream and told it to his brothers, and said, "Look, I have dreamed another dream. And this time, the sun, the moon, and the eleven stars bowed down to me."

[10] So he told *it* to his father and his brothers; and his father rebuked him and said to him, "What *is* this dream that you have dreamed? Shall your mother and I and your brothers indeed come to bow down to the earth before you?" [11] And his brothers envied him, but his father kept the matter *in mind.*

[12] Then his brothers went to feed their father's flock in Shechem. [13] And Israel said to Joseph, "Are not your brothers feeding *the flock* in Shechem? Come, I will send you to them."

So he said to him, "Here I am."

[14] Then he said to him, "Please go and see if it is well with your brothers and well with the flocks, and bring back word to me." So he sent him out of the Valley of Hebron, and he went to Shechem.

[15] Now a certain man found him, and there he was, wandering in the field. And the man asked him, saying, "What are you seeking?"

16 So he said, "I am seeking my brothers. Please tell me where they are feeding *their flocks.*"

17 And the man said, "They have departed from here, for I heard them say, 'Let us go to Dothan.'" So Joseph went after his brothers and found them in Dothan.

18 Now when they saw him afar off, even before he came near them, they conspired against him to kill him. 19 Then they said to one another, "Look, this [b]dreamer is coming! 20 Come therefore, let us now kill him and cast him into some pit; and we shall say, 'Some wild beast has devoured him.' We shall see what will become of his dreams!"

21 But Reuben heard *it,* and he delivered him out of their hands, and said, "Let us not kill him." 22 And Reuben said to them, "Shed no blood, *but* cast him into this pit which *is* in the wilderness, and do not lay a hand on him"—that he might deliver him out of their hands, and bring him back to his father.

23 So it came to pass, when Joseph had come to his brothers, that they stripped Joseph *of* his tunic, the tunic of *many* colors that *was* on him. 24 Then they took him and cast him into a pit. And the pit *was* empty; *there was* no water in it.

25 And they sat down to eat a meal. Then they lifted their eyes and looked, and there was a company of Ishmaelites, coming from Gilead with their camels, bearing spices, balm, and myrrh, on their way to carry *them* down to Egypt. 26 So Judah said to his brothers, "What profit *is there* if we kill our brother and conceal his blood? 27 Come and let us

sell him to the Ishmaelites, and let not our hand be upon him, for he *is* our brother *and* our flesh." And his brothers listened. [28] Then Midianite traders passed by; so *the brothers* pulled Joseph up and lifted him out of the pit, and sold him to the Ishmaelites for twenty *shekels* of silver. And they took Joseph to Egypt.

[29] Then Reuben returned to the pit, and indeed Joseph *was* not in the pit; and he tore his clothes. [30] And he returned to his brothers and said, "The lad *is* no *more;* and I, where shall I go?"

[31] So they took Joseph's tunic, killed a kid of the goats, and dipped the tunic in the blood. [32] Then they sent the tunic of *many* colors, and they brought *it* to their father and said, "We have found this. Do you know whether it *is* your son's tunic or not?"

[33] And he recognized it and said, "*It is* my son's tunic. A wild beast has devoured him. Without doubt Joseph is torn to pieces." [34] Then Jacob tore his clothes, put sackcloth on his waist, and mourned for his son many days. [35] And all his sons and all his daughters arose to comfort him; but he refused to be comforted, and he said, "For I shall go down into the grave to my son in mourning." Thus his father wept for him.

[36] Now the [c]Midianites had sold him in Egypt to Potiphar, an officer of Pharaoh *and* captain of the guard."

Joseph at age seventeen was only a youth yet godly. What does it say of our youth today, who seem to have set the voice of God out from their lives? Joseph had his heart in the right place. He learned from his father to read and write but also from his brother to tend his father's flock with Dan, Naphtali, Gad, and Asher. While doing this, he observed bad practice from his brothers, as in Genesis 37:2, Joseph brought back a bad report about them to his father. At this age, he was able to tell right from wrong and was willing to point this out to his father.

One day, Joseph told his brothers about his dream. His brothers interpreted the dream for themselves and became envious of him. In this age of technology, people will just push such a dream aside and call it nonsense. But these brothers knew He was talking of serious matters of leadership. They did not take His dream lightly but set out to kill him and later agreed to sell him into slavery. The story of Joseph represents a type of Christ who was humble, then exalted. It also teaches us a lot about Christians today, who must go through many tribulations before they enter into we enter into the Kingdom of God. The dreamer, Joseph, was his father's favourite, yet he was not brought up in idleness.

God prepared Joseph for his advancement but did not warn him of the persecutions to come, like Potiphar's house, or all the hardships in the prison. This happens to most people today when God gives them a dream of things to come—of a wedding or a graduation or even of heaven—but when you start going through the pain (in-laws rejecting you or perils on the way) you begin to question if the dream was indeed from God.

If God has given you a dream, He will surely find a Rueben to fight for you. Joseph is a type of Christ, and he was beloved of the Father. Just like Christ, Joseph also went ahead to preserve life.

Since we hold to the view that Joseph was a type of Christ, we can safely say that the brothers did bow to him in Egypt; yet his father and mother were not there. So who or what is the meaning of that dream for us who are not descended of Joseph. When we look at Revelation 12:1, we see a woman clothed with the sun. The sun signifies God's people in the New Testament age before Christ came to the world. The Old Testament age was the moon so both dispensations—the old and the new—bow before the King of Kings.

Before Christ came it was the age of the moon, God's people under the law of Moses. The stars represent the patriarch's people before the law was given, shining individually in the dark with divine heavenly light before the law was given. According to Daniel 12:3, God's redeemed in the Old Testament (that is, those who turn many to righteousness, who lead people to God) will shine as stars forever.

In the New Testament, believers who have received God's grace will shine much more. Paul in Philippians 2:15–16 charges us to be children of God without blemish in the midst of a crooked and perverse generation, among whom we shine. Jesus Christ is also described as the light of the world (Mathew 5:14–16).

Christ is the one we bow to, both the lesser lights (the stars and the moon) and the sun, as He is the one above all, the father of all lights. This is the full interpretation of Joseph's dream. It not only paints the picture of Israel but the picture of the Church shining in its light under Christ.

*Chapter 5*

# PHARAOH HAD A DREAM

Genesis 41:2–8

"Suddenly there came up out of the river seven cows, fine looking and fat; and they fed in the meadow. [3] Then behold, seven other cows came up after them out of the river, ugly and gaunt, and stood by the *other* cows on the bank of the river. [4] And the ugly and gaunt cows ate up the seven fine looking and fat cows. So Pharaoh awoke. [5] He slept and dreamed a second time; and suddenly seven heads of grain came up on one stalk, plump and good. [6] Then behold, seven thin heads, blighted by the east wind, sprang up after them. [7] And the seven thin heads devoured the seven plump and full heads. So Pharaoh awoke, and indeed, *it was* a dream. [8] Now it came to pass in the morning that his spirit was troubled, and he sent and called for all the magicians of Egypt and all its wise men. And Pharaoh told them his dreams, but *there was* no one who could interpret them for Pharaoh."

Why was a king bothered by dreams? Joseph was called in at the right time to interpret the dreams of Pharaoh. If the chief butler had got Joseph out of prison, he would have probably gone back to his country of origin without gaining any prominence, which had been promised to him in a dream. He would not have been a blessing at all to his father and brothers. He had been able to interpret the dreams of the baker in the prison, and now his time in the limelight had come. It was his time to honour the God of heaven and earth before Pharaoh. Somehow, God was showing humanity that He shows no partiality. He was extending grace even to those who did not yet know Him.

*Chapter 6*

# GOD PREPARES GIDEON

Judges 7:12–15

"Now the Midianites and Amalekites, all the people of the east, were lying in the valley as numerous as locusts; and their camels were without number, as the sand by the seashore in multitude. And when Gideon had come, there was a man telling a dream to his companion. He said, "I have had a dream: To my surprise, a loaf of barley bread tumbled into the camp of Midian; it came to a tent and struck it so that it fell and overturned, and the tent collapsed." Then his companion answered and said, "This is nothing else but the sword of Gideon the son of Joash, a man of Israel! Into his hand God has delivered Midian and the whole camp." And so it was, when Gideon heard the telling of the dream and its interpretation, that he worshiped. He returned to the camp of Israel, and said, "Arise, for the Lord has delivered the camp of Midian into your hand."

This passage is a very profound revelation of prophetic dreams. The person whom God chose to receive the dream was from the enemy's camp. This shows us that God speaks to anyone who is ready and willing to listen to Him. God speaks all the time, but we have made our hearing dull. Our minds are always ahead of us cluttered by the cares of each day. From this little passage we can see that God provides answers to our questions. Gideon had an army of just three hundred unskilled warriors, but the enemy's camp had numerous gallant soldiers, experienced in warfare. This he saw as a great challenge. He was probably overloaded with questions: How was he going to attack such a big army? How could he arrange the three hundred men? So many questions other soldiers asked him, but he could not reassure them. He had one thing, however—the only thing—his trust in the Lord. Sometimes when we get to that place where we cannot see beyond the challenge, God communicates in prophetic dreams.

In their eyes, the army of Israel was small (inferior) compared to their massive, well-trained enemy. Barley represented agriculture, and the Israelites engaged in this form of livelihood. The tent represented the whole Midianite camp. The use of the tent suggests the Midianites' nomadic lifestyle.

This dream encouraged Gideon, and he worshipped God. There are dreams that God gives us just to encourage us, so it is well after we dream to enter into a time of worship.

*Chapter 7*

# SOLOMON

Solomon was one of the wisest kings who ever lived on this earth. He was the son of David by Bathsheba, the wife of Uriah. Solomon had been raised by a wise king and had watched him rule God's people in love and wisdom. His reign was between 970 BC to 931 BC.

One of the teachings from Proverbs 4:7 says,

"Wisdom *is* the principal thing; *Therefore* get wisdom. And in all your getting, get understanding."

David had passed on to his son a desire and thirst for eternal motives. He advised him to acquire wisdom despite all cost. Proverbs calls it the principal thing of value, which great men who change the world cannot do without.

Knowledge is the accumulation of information, but wisdom is the understanding, grasping, comprehension, and interpretation of that information. It is the ability to apply the information. Wisdom is the top priority on the list of our wants.

In this day of the Internet and social media, there is information everywhere. Facebook, Twitter, WhatsApp, and other media services share vast amounts of information about health, wealth, politics, and other matters relating to our world today, but in this, there is no wisdom.

The more knowledge there is, the more moral decay. If most of us exercised wisdom and discernment instead of following every idea flowing through our world today, we could work with such foresight and insight and stem the tide of foolishness that has covered the earth in the age of knowledge. Without wisdom, knowledge is dangerous. Just because we can do something doesn't mean we should do it.

> 1 Kings 3:5–15
>
> "At Gibeon the Lord appeared to Solomon in a dream by night; and God said, "Ask! What shall I give you?"
>
> [6] And Solomon said: "You have shown great mercy to Your servant David my father, because he walked before You in truth, in righteousness, and in uprightness of heart with You; You have continued this great kindness for him, and You have given him a son to sit on his throne, as *it is* this day. [7] Now, O Lord my God, You have made Your servant king instead of my father David, but I *am* a little child; I do not know *how* to go out or come in. [8] And Your servant *is* in the midst of Your people whom You have chosen, a great people, too numerous to be numbered or counted. [9] Therefore give to Your servant an [b]understanding heart to judge Your people, that I may discern between

good and evil. For who is able to judge this great people of Yours?"

[10] The speech pleased the Lord, that Solomon had asked this thing. [11] Then God said to him: "Because you have asked this thing, and have not asked long life for yourself, nor have asked riches for yourself, nor have asked the life of your enemies, but have asked for yourself understanding to discern justice, [12] behold, I have done according to your words; see, I have given you a wise and understanding heart, so that there has not been anyone like you before you, nor shall any like you arise after you. [13] And I have also given you what you have not asked: both riches and honor, so that there shall not be anyone like you among the kings all your days. [14] So if you walk in My ways, to keep My statutes and My commandments, as your father David walked, then I will lengthen[c] your days."

[15] Then Solomon awoke; and indeed it had been a dream. And he came to Jerusalem and stood before the ark of the covenant of the Lord, offered up burnt offerings, offered peace offerings, and made a feast for all his servants.

Solomon had a conversation with the Lord in a dream. We as believers can train our spirit to hear the voice of God at all times whether we are awake or asleep. God chose to speak to Moses face to face, but to Solomon, He chose to speak to him in a dream. Solomon encounteres God in a vivid dream, where God spoke and Solomon spoke. There was a clear interaction. At that time, Solomon was about twenty years old and inexperienced at governing God's people. Inexperience in discerning between right and wrong, and at that, the king in Israel had a judiciary role. He also had to act as a judge to God's people. Solomon needed God's guidance in exercising authority over God's people. He also realised that God is the true lawgiver and the source of all wisdom and knowledge. God was pleased with Solomon's request and it was granted. He made him the wisest man that ever lived, giving him riches, honour, and long life. When God made Solomon wise in a dream, the manifestation of the wisdom was seen by all people. For example, there is a story of the two prostitutes who were in the same house, and one carelessly killed her baby while she slept. When she discovered what she had done, she swapped the babies. The next day, the other one inspected her child and found that it was not hers. The two went to King Solomon to determine who the mother of the baby was. Solomon decided he would cut the living baby, to be shared between the two of them. When the mother heard this, she cried to the king and said, "Let the other women have the child, but spare his life." From this, Solomon rightly discerned who the real mother was. When all Israel heard this, they knew that this wisdom came from God.

David had his communication with God through prophets such as Nathan, Gad, and Samuel. But Solomon is in another dimension, as God came to speak to him personally in a dream. It must be noted that it is God who chooses, by talking to a prophet, through a waking vision, or in a night dream. There is no inferior method.

God always responds to an inward desire to hear from Him. Solomon had a thirst for God. Hence, God came in a dream and met his desire for more wisdom through a dream. So we know in these last days that the youth who desire to meet God will meet with Him through dreams.

*Chapter 8*

# DREAMS INSTRUCTING DISCIPLES

Paul's dramatic conversion is considered to be one of the two great proofs of the validity of the Christian faith, the other being the resurrection of Christ. Paul had an encounter with the living God on his way to Damascus to persecute the saints. Paul met Christ on his way to a religious mission. In his own eyes he was serving God the best way he knew how. He had a passion to see all men follow the way of his father, according to the Jewish teachings. Anything out of this faith was heresy, and anyone polluting the nation with any ideology apart from Judaism had to die. Paul earnestly believed he was doing the right thing; he probably saw himself as Elijah, anointed to purge Israel from false religion. He did not realise that he was not just persecuting people but Christ himself (Acts 9:1–18).

"Then Saul, still breathing threats and murder against the disciples of the Lord, went to the high priest [2] and asked letters from him to the synagogues of Damascus, so that if he found any who were of the Way, whether men or women, he might bring them bound to Jerusalem.

³ As he journeyed he came near Damascus, and suddenly a light shone around him from heaven. ⁴ Then he fell to the ground, and heard a voice saying to him, "Saul, Saul, why are you persecuting Me?"

⁵ And he said, "Who are You, Lord?"

Then the Lord said, "I am Jesus, whom you are persecuting. [a]It *is* hard for you to kick against the goads."

⁶ So he, trembling and astonished, said, "Lord, what do You want me to do?"

Then the Lord *said* to him, "Arise and go into the city, and you will be told what you must do."

⁷ And the men who journeyed with him stood speechless, hearing a voice but seeing no one. ⁸ Then Saul arose from the ground, and when his eyes were opened he saw no one. But they led him by the hand and brought *him* into Damascus. ⁹ And he was three days without sight, and neither ate nor drank.

¹⁰ Now there was a certain disciple at Damascus named Ananias; and to him the Lord said in a vision, "Ananias."

And he said, "Here I am, Lord."

¹¹ So the Lord *said* to him, "Arise and go to the street called Straight, and inquire at the house of Judas for *one* called Saul of Tarsus, for behold, he is praying. ¹² And in a vision he has seen a man named Ananias coming in and putting *his* hand on him, so that he might receive his sight."

¹³ Then Ananias answered, "Lord, I have heard from many about this man, how much [b]harm he has done to Your saints in Jerusalem. ¹⁴ And here he has authority from the chief priests to bind all who call on Your name."

[15] But the Lord said to him, "Go, for he is a chosen vessel of Mine to bear My name before Gentiles, kings, and the children[c] of Israel. [16] For I will show him how many things he must suffer for My name's sake."

[17] And Ananias went his way and entered the house; and laying his hands on him he said, "Brother Saul, the Lord [d]Jesus, who appeared to you on the road as you came, has sent me that you may receive your sight and be filled with the Holy Spirit." [18] Immediately there fell from his eyes *something* like scales, and he received his sight at once; and he arose and was baptized."

Jesus appeared to both Paul and Ananias. Ananias was understandably reluctant to receive Paul because of what he knew about Saul. God used a dream to instruct Annanais on what to do when Saul came over. Saul of Tarsus received the Holy Spirit as a result of Ananias receiving instruction in a vision. He obeyed God and laid hands on one who was once an enemy of the Gospel. More miracles happened, Saul was changed to Paul then his sight was restored praise the Lord all this because men took heed of dreams.

> Joel 2:28, Acts 2v 17 NKJV
> 'And it shall come to pass in the last days, says God,
> That I will pour out of My Spirit on all flesh;
> Your sons and your daughters shall prophesy,
> Your young men shall see visions,
> Your old men shall dream dreams.

Acts 2:17 points out to the phenomenon of this experience: "and it shall come to pass in the last days, says God, that I will pour out my spirit on all flesh; your sons and your daughters shall prophesy. Your young men shall see visions and your old men shall dream dreams." The "last days" refers to the era of the Church from the Pentecost to the return of Christ. Hebrews 1:1 points out that God speaks. "He has done this in the past, and He speaks today." God spoke to prophets in Daniel 2:3 and Ezekiel 8:4: "He speaks in various ways, and these ways included dreams and visions." Peter made reference to the prophetic word by Joel. The last days are marked by an outpouring of God's spirit upon all flesh, including Gentiles from all walks of life —Hindus, Moslems, Buddhists, the religious and the non-religious. God will pour out His spirit with only one goal: to harvest souls from darkness to light, from death to life, from a lost eternity to salvation of souls.

Peter explains the unusual events of Pentecost regarding the prediction of Joel in his Messianic prophecy. In the Old Testament, the anointing of the Holy Spirit had been largely reserved for the spiritual and national leaders of Israel. Under the new era or new covenant, however, the Spirit is for those that receive him John 1:12. Every believer is anointed to be a priest and a king under God. Important evidence of participation in the Spirit outpouring is dreams and prophecies.

## The Story of Cornelius

The story of Cornelius is one of the examples of where God has visited non-Jewish people:

Acts 10:1-2

"There was a certain man in Caesarea called Cornelius, a centurion of what was called the Italian [a] Regiment, [2] a devout *man* and one who feared God with all his household, who gave [b]alms generously to the people, and prayed to God always."

Cornelius was a Gentile who earnestly desired to know God. He prayed and also gave to the poor. One of the true marks of a follower of Christ is compassion. The Bible tells us that Jesus Christ went about doing good. This man was full of good works, and his actions drew God's attention. God appeared to him in a vision and gave him instructions (Acts 10:5-9).

## Peter

Acts 10:48

Peter went to pray. Then, in a trance, he saw the heavens open. The Greek word for trance is "ecstasy", which stems from the word *existerni*, meaning displacement of the ordinary state of mind with an elevated, God-given state of mind, in this case to instruct him. This is in line with the prophetic promise of dreams and visions in Acts 2:17, given by the Holy Spirit to advance God's redemptive purposes. Three times Peter saw a vision of ritually unclean animals, and each time a heavenly voice insisted that he eat them in violation of Jewish traditions and beliefs.

The triple dream was intended to show Peter that God is not a respecter of persons. Peter would have not visited Cornelius, a Gentile and an opponent of the Jewish establishment. At this point, Peter does not yet realise that God wants everyone, regardless of their nationality or ethnic orientation, to hear the good news of the Gospel and believe in Christ, the only way to salvation. Peter's bias was confronted with a vision, and this is the biblical school of the Holy Spirit.

God can use dreams to instruct us on the way. In the book of Matthew (1:20-24), Joseph is instructed in a dream not to put Mary away. God gives divine direction to Joseph in a dream. God knows Mary cannot survive in that culture as a single mother; it was therefore important that Joseph receive instructions on how to raise the Christ of God as a child.

The household of the Gentile Cornelius was included in the outpouring of the Holy Spirit, according to the prophecy of Joel 2:28. God is still calling people in the same way. The Church has to begin to harness this great outpouring and not restrict the movement of God through hostility to dreams and visions.

## The Macedonian Call

Acts 1:9

Macedonia was the northern part of Greece. The Holy Spirit communicated and directed the missionaries on God's agenda through a dream. Many people today speak of dreams of preaching in foreign nations. A young brother in the Lord came to tell me that he often dreams of preaching in India. After many dreams, he set off to India and God provided miraculously. When he got to India, he opened an orphanage and started preaching to the locals.

We need to take heed of prophetic dreams. If the apostles obeyed the instructions passed on to them in dreams, the end time Church ought to do the same.

We find that in prophetic dreams, God warns us of unseen danger. He warned Joseph to leave Israel for a while to go and live in Egypt. He also guides us from wrongdoing (e.g., Genesis 20:3–8). Joseph was visited by an angel in a dream to prepare him for what was happening with Mary, not to put her away. The angel reminded him that Mary carried the seed of the Holy Spirit. In the book of Matthew (2:13-15), we see Joseph being warned to take Mary and the child into Egypt until Herods death.

## God Gives Us Supernatural Gifts in Dreams

The Lord appeared to Solomon in a dream and said, "Ask what I shall give you" (1Kings 3:5-9)(verse 9). "So give your servant a heart of wisdom so I can govern your people and to distinguish between right and wrong, for who is able to govern this great people of yours?" (verse 12). "I will do what you have asked (13–15)." If the devil can give affliction and initiate people into witchcraft while men sleep, God does the opposite—(He)he blesses people, giving them skills, long life, and blessings in a dream.

Don't miss out. Ask Him to visit you as you as you sleep and (ask Him to) deposit in you the eternal gift.

*Chapter 9*

# HOW TO CAPTURE DREAMS

Before you go to bed, prepare yourself to hear messages from the Lord. It is advisable to keep a dream journal. Keep a book and pen next to you as you go to bed, and once you wake up, write the dream. Everyone can learn and develop their own dream language. People have different backgrounds, cultures, educations, and professional standings. We are not all at the same spiritual level, so our dream language will differ from one person to another. While I have put down a few interpretations and symbols, I strongly discourage dream dictionaries, because God deals with us as individuals and wants to take us from where we are.

If we are to receive instruction from the Lord, we must stay away from stimulants, drugs, sleeping tablets, and too much food at night. Do not use an alarm to wake up. Ask the Holy Spirit to wake you up. Write down everything you can remember about the dream—the people, animals, plants, colours, and your emotions. These will help in the interpretation of the dreams. Compare the symbols with what is written in the word of God. Pray and ask God to help you with the meaning. The Holy Spirit will help you interpret the numbers, colours, etc. Think about your emotions, as this will also help with the interpretation. Think of this. Were you:

- happy?
- crying?
- tearful?
- angry?
- aggressive?
- fighting?
- running?
- afraid?

What figure were you drawn to? Is anything related to your current life events, people, or family? Is anything related to the past? What happened to you and hurt your emotions? If that is the case, pray and ask God to heal you of your past. You may need to forgive siblings, parents, friends, church members, and pastors.

Ask if this dream is about now or the future. Does it affect only you or other people around you? Are you the central figure in the dream, or are there other key people? Is it about you or other people? Do you feel it's about other people? Ask God to give you wisdom so you do not go about offending people, giving them dreams that put fear in them. For instance, if you dream of someone dying, you cannot go and tell them they are going to die, as the dream might actually mean something totally different. It may mean cutting ties with that person or that they are going to experience a death of self and live completely separated from the Lord.

If you are under a lot of stress or extremely busy, your dreams may be influenced by such. The political/economic discussion of the day may affect us. Today, most people are genuinely concerned about Brexit and its effect on human lives. The discussion appears regularly on TV debates. If we spend a lot of time listening to such matters that have a direct effect on us, we may end up dreaming about them. We should not take every dream as a message from God. It may not be necessary to keep stressing over such dreams.

When you have a dream, pray before you utter meaning; before you hurt people. If God is saying something, pray and ask God what He is trying to say to you. Don't ignore dreams when you think they are too difficult to understand. Keep asking God for a full answer. Sometimes a dream is an answer to questions we have asked God.

Sometimes God shows us naked people. We may not be in the position to tell them this, but pray for God to cover them, as nakedness may mean shame in other cultures. We should always link up our dreams to the word of God. After a dream, ask yourself what the Bible says about the kind of word, symbol, colour, or number you encountered. Get enough sleep (at least 8 hours) if you want to dream.

# Chapter 10

# SOME DREAMS

A woman suffering from cancer lived in my house for about six months. We used to have time to pray together and study the word of God. She was a lovely Christian woman who had done a lot in the Church of God. She was in the process of writing some books for publication. One day, she woke up and asked me to interpret her dream. She told me she had had a beautiful dream where she saw seven young boys standing in front of her. She was very happy and interpreted the dream to mean that God would allow her to complete her seven books before she died. We prayed together about the dream, and I got a very different meaning from the one above. After praying with her and seeking God for the meaning of the dream, I told her that God was giving her seven days to live and she needed to forgive her family members.

For the following seven days, we called her family in Nigeria and the UK, and she had an opportunity to speak to all those people. On the last day, the seventh day, she asked after one family member who had not responded to her call. After more prayer, that family member was on the phone.

That night, as I slept, I had a dream that someone was speaking to me. I was told they could remove sickness from a body or remove a person from a sick body—either way, it was a healing blessing. I woke up and saw that there was no one talking to me. When I called the hospital, I heard that my friend had gone to be with the Lord. To God be the glory. Here is one that God prepared through a dream.

## Another Dream

Around August 2017, I had a dream. I was in a church, and many people were honouring one another. They would give these elaborate greetings, welcoming each other as Doctor, Archbishop, Apostle, and various other grand titles. They would clap hands for each other and celebrate their achievements in education and material acquisitions.

The place was a big, well-decorated auditorium, and the people were well-decorated and well-dressed also. I started to feel out of place and got angry that there was no mention of Jesus Christ and no preaching, only honouring of men. Towards the exit, I saw a small group of people standing obliviously, not interested in what was going on in this big church. I walked toward them, and we stood in a small group of about ten individuals. Above us the roof appeared open. We could see the blue sky above us. Something fascinating began to happen. A big eagle-like bird swooped down and caught a chick. It was about to fly off with the chick when a brown hen flew up in chase of the eagle. It fought to recover its chick. I looked at it, and in my heart I thought, *A chicken is no match for an eagle. There is no way it will recover that chick.* As the eagle flew higher, I saw the brown chicken pursuing the eagle and fighting to recover the chick. The fight was vicious, and in the end, the chicken recovered its chick. The few of us started shouting, "Yes, it has recovered. Yes, it has recovered."

When I woke up, I was disturbed by the dream and wanted to know the meaning, so I prayed. I asked God to tell me what it meant. Generally speaking, I love the eagle, as it is related to godly things in many ways, and I did not understand why a chicken would overpower an eagle (I will not preach about the eagle, because of the many falsehoods preached by Pentecostal Pastors about the eagle). I also wondered if the Bible had anything to say about chickens. Then I got this scripture from Matthew 23:37: "Jerusalem, you who kill the prophets and stone those sent to you, how often I have longed to gather your children together as a hen gathers her chicks under her wings …"

Jesus was lamenting on their hypocrisy and was grief-stricken over Jerusalem. Christ's last words before (He)he died were a lament over the spiritual situation of Israel. He was lamenting over the leaders, denouncing their hypocrisy. Today, it's the same. His heart is broken by the Churchianity going on. The Church looks like that giant eagle professing to have power and authority and majesty. The chicken, on the other hand, represents a vulnerable, common group of people who have a godly burden and mandate to recover what has been lost through religion,

Churchianity, and hypocrisy. This group of people are common. They do not have big names. They probably are not known, yet they possess in them the disdain for religion and are ready to recover the apostolic age. The Lord warned me that was not an eagle but a symbol and that was not a chicken but a symbol.

My prayer from that day was, "Lord, raise your end time army that can recover the apostolic age and prepare your Church for the coming revivals." God is going to raise the unknown, uncelebrated of our day to do extraordinary work for (Him)him. Just like the chicken, they look common, yet they possess qualities to fight and take what the church has lost.

## Chapter 11

# PROPHETIC DREAMS

## The Book Of Daniel

In a prophetic <u>dream,</u> you see the future through your dreams. It may take longer to establish that what was seen is prophetic, as it will take years to come to pass. Daniel did not live long enough to see the manifestation of his dreams in Daniel 7. In these dreams, Daniel describes four beasts coming up from the Mediterranean Sea. Daniel 7:7: "After this I saw in the night visions and behold a fourth beast dreadful and terrible, exceedingly strong."

The vision predicts major world empires and events from the time of Daniel to the second coming of Christ. The vision ended with Daniel saying, my thoughts greatly troubled me, and my countenance changed; but I kept the matter in my heart." The dreams in Daniel 2 were interpreted by Daniel in a vision by God to refer to the four successive empires of Babylon, Medo/Persian, Greek and Roman.

There are two main reasons to show us that these first four empires are not the same as the empires described as beasts in Daniel 7.

1. Daniel 7:1 says

"In the first year of Belshazzar king of Babylon, Daniel [a]had a dream and visions of his head *while* on his bed. Then he wrote down the dream, telling [b]the main facts.

If therefore this dream by Daniel was in the year of Belshazzar king of Babylon, then it could not be a dream prophesying the coming of the Babylonian Empire, which came with Nebopolassar the father of King Nebucchadnezzar. In any case, Belshazzar died soon after and the empire was taken over by the Medes.

2. Daniel 2:40-45

"And the fourth kingdom shall be as strong as iron, inasmuch as iron breaks in pieces and shatters everything; and like iron that crushes, *that kingdom* will break in pieces and crush all the others. [41] Whereas you saw the feet and toes, partly of potter's clay and partly of iron, the kingdom shall be divided; yet the strength of the iron shall be in it, just as you saw the iron mixed with ceramic clay. [42] And *as* the toes of the feet *were* partly of iron and partly of clay, *so* the kingdom shall be partly strong and partly [m]fragile. [43] As you saw iron mixed with ceramic clay, they will mingle with the seed of men; but they will not adhere to one another, just as iron does not mix with clay. [44] And in the days of these kings the God of heaven will set up a kingdom which shall never be destroyed; and the kingdom shall not be left to other people; it shall [n]break in pieces and [o]consume all these kingdoms, and it shall stand forever. [45] Inasmuch as you saw that the stone was cut out of the mountain without hands, and that it broke in pieces the iron, the bronze, the clay, the silver, and the gold—the great God has made known to the king what will come to pass after this. The dream is certain, and its interpretation is sure."

It is clear that the fourth empire of Daniel 2 is the Roman Empire. It is also clear that Daniel is shown in the interpretation the coming of the Kingdom of God and that the Roman Empire and its Holy Roman Empire are going to be destroyed completely. Most importantly Daniel 2 prophesies that Christianity shall not be destroyed by any other empire on earth.

The dream in Daniel 7 prophesies of the end times. The symbols used in the dream are consistent with characteristics of the world empires that we have seen in the last five centuries.

Daniel 7:3 says

"And four great beasts came up from the sea, each different from the other. [4] The first *was* like a lion, and had eagle's wings. I watched till its wings were plucked off; and it was lifted up from the earth and made to stand on two feet like a man, and a man's heart was given to it."

The first world empire that we have seen in the past five centuries is the Anglo/American alliance. The emblem of the British empire is the lion and the emblem of the American States is the eagle. In the last fifty years this alliance has been losing its grip on world power through decolonisation.

Daniel 7:5

"And suddenly another beast, a second, like a bear. It was raised up on one side, and *had* three ribs in its mouth between its teeth. And they said thus to it: 'Arise, devour much flesh!'"

The Soviet Union and the Russian Federation are known in the world as "The Bear". It is a brutal regime which exerted its world power through surrogates. From the 1920's it supplied weapons to world revolutions and rebel organisations and was responsible for the killings of many people the world over. Even now it still sells one of the most dangerous guerrilla weapons the world has ever known- the AK47 rifle.

Daniel 7:6

"After this I looked, and there was another, like a leopard, which had on its back four wings of a bird. The beast also had four heads, and dominion was given to it."

This empire denotes the Chinese control of world affairs. This empire is unfolding right before our eyes right now. There are three features that point tro this world empire being the Chinese world empire:-

The leopard is significant because of its yellowish brownish colour, which is the skin colour of the Chinese. The wings denote the speed with which the Chinese will conquer the whole world in a very short space of time. The leopard is a very fast animal on land, and you can imagine if it has wings as well. Lastly the Chinese has not fired a single shot in taking over the world. Many factories in America, Europe, Africa and the rest of the world closed because they could not compete with Chinese products. Dominion was given to this animal and we see all countries falling all over themselves to do business with China.

Europe and America owe China trillions upon trillions of dollars. African countries are literally owned by China, and again all this without China fighting a single battle to gain all this world wealth.

Daniel 7:7-8

"After this I saw in the night visions, and behold, a fourth beast, dreadful and terrible, exceedingly strong. It had huge iron teeth; it was devouring, breaking in pieces, and trampling the residue with its feet. It *was* different from all the beasts that *were* before it, and it had ten horns. [8] I was considering the horns, and there was another horn, a little one, coming up among them, before whom three of the first horns were plucked out by the roots. And there, in this horn, *were* eyes like the eyes of a man, and a mouth speaking [c]pompous words."

This last beast takes power from all the beasts. This same beast is described in Revelation 13

"Then [a]I stood on the sand of the sea. And I saw a beast rising up out of the sea, having [b]seven heads and ten horns, and on his horns ten crowns, and on his heads a blasphemous name. [2] Now the beast which I saw was like a leopard, his feet were like *the feet of* a bear, and his mouth like the mouth of a lion. The dragon gave him his power, his throne, and great authority."

Rising up from the sea denotes that it is a creation of mankind, because in the Bible water represents people and the sea represents the world population. Genesis

49:4; Isaiah 57:20; Jude 12-13. This is a political system that will be accepted by all countries of the world, much like Democracy. All world governments are accepting democracy, even China is marching towards democracy.

The significance of pompous words spoken by this beast, in my opinion, refers to the blasphemy of politics. In fact other versions say speaking great blasphemies. We have democracy today pushing all the countries of the world to accept what they call "human rights". But these "human rights" are contrary to the word of God: homosexuality, abortion, adultery, incest, paedophilia, smoking of ganja, banning of the bible and Lord's Prayer from schools and government institutions, insubordination of children to their parents, etc. Daniel was being shown in a vision what the world has come to be today and this is why he said that his thoughts troubled him.

Daniel's dreams are prophetic, pointing to the future of mankind. He had the joyful prospect of the prevalence of God's kingdom among men. This refers to the second coming of our blessed Lord Jesus Christ, when the saints shall triumph in the complete fall of Satan's kingdom. The saints of the most high shall possess the kingdom forever. This dream speaks of God's promises that the gospel kingdom shall be set up—a kingdom of light, holiness, and love, a kingdom of grace and privileges and comforts, which shall be earnest and have the first fruits of the Kingdom of Glory. The full accomplishment will be in the happiness of the saints, the kingdom that cannot be moved, the gathering together of the whole family of God under Christ's rule.

In the Abrahamic covenant (Genesis 15:1), God promised Abraham he would be a father to many nations. While Abraham lived, he had sons Isaac and Ismail and a few others from (Keturah, Genesis 25:1-6). It was in Abraham's death that the promise was fulfilled in Christ, bringing many into the kingdom through his death. The natural children of Abraham are those Jewish and Arabic (Ishmaelite's) children, and the stars of heaven are those from every nation upon the earth who have received Christ and become children of Abraham by faith.

*Chapter 12*

# RELATING DREAMS TO PHYSICAL CONDITIONS

Dreams can help us diagnose the causes of our physical and mental ailments.

Some time ago I was praying for people who were unwell. A man came to tell me he had spent years enduring a difficult, oppressive condition. He had become so unwell that he had to leave work. I asked him to describe his illness and why he had not gone for medical help. The man explained that doctors had done many tests on him, but every blood test, urine test, whatever test, had come back negative, yet this wonderful man could not sleep. He explained that he felt some animals moving in his body. This caused him to lose sleep, and he stayed up all night and was desperate to get well. I asked further if he was married, and he said he had been single for 15 years after the death of his wife. After further questions, I asked if he remembered any dreams at all. Then he told me, "Oh, yes." For the past 15 years, his wife had come to have sex and he remembered that from the first time they had sex, these problems started. He was not willing to let go, as he loved his wife.

After showing him a few scriptures (Ecclesiastes 9:5) "For the living know that they will die; But the dead know nothing. And they have no more reward, For the memory of them is forgotten." They no longer, have a part to play in our lives now either to love us or hate (bring) punishment.

We were able to pray and break those lies from the enemy. I encouraged this man to start praying for himself and feeding his spirit with the word of God. After much prayer, this man was set free and went back to work, married a beautiful wife, and served the Lord.


## A Young Girl

A young girl had severe chest pains and occasional fainting. They would rush her to the hospital with various ailments, each time coming back with a prescription for simple painkillers. The mother of this 11-year-old girl was concerned about her deteriorating health and called me to pray for this young person. A friend of mine and I went over to pray for this young person. I asked this girl to tell me what her dreams were like. She went on to say that she had a recurring dream where a woman she knew fed her rotten food. We encouraged her to give her heart to the Lord and pray over her, cutting her off from these re-curring dreams. Today this young girl has a good job, drives a good car, and is no longer tormented. Praise God!

**A Friend's Dream**

A friend of mine went to have time in the presence of the Lord. This is what she does at the beginning of each year: she goes away for a month to Kenya to pray for her ministry and the body of Christ. She wrote this in her book *Character Matches the Assignment* (page 39). She went to Kenya to pray and fast, and this is her story:

> "First day in Kenya. The Lord's presence in the room was tangible, and all I could see was the state of my heart. I didn't like what I saw, but I will try my best to describe it to you because, who knows, you might be going through the same things with no idea of what to do. I saw a heart that had so many holes in it, ragged wounds, like gunshot wounds. Some of the wound were gangrenous in colour, some were yellowish, and some were still bleeding. What amazed me the most was that the wounds were dated and named after those I held responsible for my broken heart. I asked the Lord if he could explain to me what was this all about.
>
> The Lord answered, "The state of your heart is not looking good. A heart like this cannot hold my mysteries." My heart actually could not retain anything. You can choose to have it mended."

The entire dream led my friend to see the need to forgive people who have hurt her in the past and God used a dream to bring back her child to a place of restoration, newness, and joy. This woman of God walks in the zeal and fire of God, with evidence of walking in great love for God and people around her.

*Chapter 13*

# NIGHTMARES

Psychological triggers can cause nightmares in adults. For example, anxiety and depression can cause adult nightmares. Post-traumatic stress disorder also commonly causes people to experience chronic recurrent nightmares. Nightmares in adults can be caused by certain sleep disorders.

WebMD (www.webmd.com) says that nightmares are common among adults and one out of two adults has nightmares. They cause distress and interrupt sleep, but we need to look at what causes them. One other source describes nightmares as vivid, realistic, disturbing dreams that rattle you awake from a deep sleep. They often set your heart pounding with fear. Nightmares tend to occur most often during the rapid eye movement (REM) sleep, when most disturbing dreaming takes place. Periods of REM sleep become progressively longer as the night progresses.

Some common nightmares include not being able to run fast enough to escape danger or being about to fall from a great height or drown in a river.

Scientists try to explain some causes of nightmares. Among others are the following reasons.

- Eating late at night can cause nightmares because of increased metabolism and brain activity.
- Medication and drugs can affect chemicals in the brain.
- Withdrawal from alcohol and medication can cause nightmares.

One day, when I was on the ward, a woman was sleeping, and she started screaming. She was so loud that two nurses came to her aid. She was screaming, "Get off me, you old wicked man." And when the nurses got there, she was punching in the air and screaming. We watched the process, and we did not wake her up. We could not wake her up from the nightmare because she was responding to unseen things. When the nightmare was over, she explained to us that an ugly old man was chasing her and was trying to suffocate her. She was sweating and very fearful, but after a while, she realised that it was a nightmare.

Nightmares are real. These are spiritual encounters. Just as God visits people to inspire them, the devil also as a counterfeit brings terror and torment in the sleep. He takes advantage of people's weakness in their sleep.

Psalm 91:5: "You will not fear the terror of the night, Nor the arrow that flies by the day."

We as children of God we are protected by the Most High God. He is our refuge, our fortress, and our strong tower. His angels watch over us at night. We are spiritual beings, and the devil operates in the spiritual realm. We have no power to protect ourselves when we are asleep, but God has promised us in His word that His security is over those who fear His name, and He has given assurance that we have no reason to fear. If these nightmares are consistent or they persist in our lives, one could end up losing their mind.

Despite being branded as nightmares, such dreams can also happen during the day, because they are a spiritual phenomenon. Some people will avoid going to bed at night, but this does not resolve the issue. Repeated nightmares can lead someone to mental depression, and one needs to find a way of resolving this matter through prayer. One needs to assess their own spiritual life and question what doors they have opened to allow such spiritual activity. Doors to the enemy can be opened through sin, through watching horror movies, or reading demonic material. This gives the enemy a foothold and a legal right to oppress the victim. Some traditional occult practices also open doors to the enemy, like tarot cards, ouiji boards, palm reading, acupuncture, reflexology, yoga, and freemasonry. I have just listed a few, but there are many more occult practices that the enemy uses to trap and contaminate us people.

The way to come out of all this is prayer—using the word of God and memorising scripture to do with the blood of Jesus Christ. You must be able to call on the blood of Jesus Christ even in one's sleep.

## Witchcraft Contamination in Dreams

Many African people have testified how some have been initiated into witchcraft through dreams, for example, when one dreams they are being fed raw meat or offered to drink blood. Once this happens, the spirit of man is contaminated. One is part of darkness and a part of witchcraft.

The story of Matthew (13:24-30) involving tares being sown while men slept has been translated by others to mean that the devil does not sleep when men sleep but takes advantage of their point of weakness and sows all sorts of evil. The enemy has an evil agenda and at any time will push this upon those who sleep. The Bible teaches us to watch and pray even in our sleep. If we practice calling on the name of Jesus Christ and teaching our spirit and soul to be saturated by the word of God, we will be able even in our sleep to call out the word of God to ward off attacks and plays of the enemy.

People have dreamt they were eating unusual objects like charcoal, black or red, clay, human waste, fermented or decaying meat, and maggots. Many of these things are an initiation into witchcraft, or people are being directly poisoned. They wake up and find out they suffer health problems, including mental illness, hallucinations, migraines, and unexplainable health conditions.

Some people have repeated dreams that lead them to depression and suicide. Some people who are going through addictions, love, or violent behaviours have traced those habits to dreams they have had.

## A Boy Called Tee

A young boy of 15 had a terrible experience recently. He had a dream that he was having fun with a beautiful girl, and later in the dream, he saw the girl turned herself into a beetle. He woke feeling strange. He asked to go to the bathroom and spent more than one and a half hours scrubbing himself from top to bottom, believing he had bugs all over his body. He came out of the bathroom terrified of bugs all over the room. He could not put on shoes, as they were full of bugs. I immediately sensed in my spirit that this was a spiritual matter and began to pray in the spirit, binding those demons of hallucination and confusion.

The young man was encouraged to pray. In the next few days, he was completely set free. It is indeed true that the enemy visits people while they sleep and causes them to partake in witchcraft assignments or poisons their physical bodies, causing untold suffering. Many people have prayed after having such strange dreams, and God has set them free.

We have to watch ourselves. Some people eat freely in their dreams. Most of the time when you are offered food in your dream, it is targeted at making you lose something—your health, a breakthrough, or an initiation into witchcraft. If such dreams persist, then you need deliverance.

I am not a person who likes to tell people how they can pray, as I believe prayer is an intimate conversation between you and your loving Father. However, I have one simple prayer that I encourage people to pray if they are under demonic attack. After praying and thanking the Lord for the day, I make this simple declaration:

> Lords Jesus Christ
> Make my bones red hot pillars of fire
> Make my flesh red-hot coals of fire
> Make my blood red hot rivers of fire
> I am a flame of fire
> Satan and his demons cannot touch me
> I am a flame of fire
> Satan cannot touch this fire
> My God is a consuming fire, and His fire
> surrounds me.

Everyone can make their own prayer in their own language. It is important to know that this prayer only works when you have a relationship with the Lord and you are not walking or living in sin.

Some people like to go for deliverance, and I will caution you not to go to false prophets for this, but go to a humble man, your pastor or Elder. I know Jesus Christ is the one to deliver men from bondage, whether you decide to have someone pray for you or you pray on your own. It's not the noise or the title of man that delivers, but Christ Jesus himself can set you free from bondages of witchcraft.

If we can stop these demonic dreams from taking place in our lives, we learn to live a prayerful life that is directed by the eating of God's word. Read the word in the morning and just before going to bed. Memorise a scripture before closing your eyes to sleep. If you realise you have a habit of eating in your dreams, then go on a fast if possible—an absolute fast. Many people have been set free after fasting; they vomit charcoal-like substances or pass it through as black faeces. It is commendable to tell God everything, to repent of your eating and have Him set you free from bondage.

Another way of getting yourself clean is by taking Holy Communion and declaring the healing that flows from the blood of Jesus Christ. As children of God, we know we can pull out our weapons of war from our royal arsenal. The greatest weapon given to the church is the name of Jesus.

Philippians (2:10) says "that at the name of Jesus every knee should bow of those in heaven, and of those on earth, and of those under the earth" and (verse 11) "that every tongue should confess that Jesus Christ is Lord, to the glory of God the Father."

The second weapon we pull out is the blood of Jesus Christ. Once contamination occurs through eating in our dreams, we can cry out for the blood of Jesus Christ to wash over us. In the Old Testament, God took great care to teach His people that the cleansing could only be through the blood. This was the meaning of every smoking altar and the rivers of blood that flowed from the Jewish altars. On the dark night when Israel left Egypt, blood played a big part in their deliverance. In the twelfth chapter of the book of Exodus 12:21-28, we have a full description of the slaying of the Passover lamb and the sprinkling of the blood. The Christ we serve was without spot or blemish. We are privileged to know that His blood is the one that can set us free from all forms of contamination.

1 Corinthians 1:30 says, "But of Him you are in Christ Jesus, who became for us wisdom from God-and righteousness and sanctification and redemption."

You are complete in Him Col 2:10. Our sanctification is in Him, Christ is made unto us sanctification. He gives u2s his heart, His mind, His holiness, His indwelling life to keep us pure and holy. Christ is made to our redemption. The word redemption has a larger meaning than our mind can conceive. It not only means deliverance from sin in its two-fold nature, but redemption in Christ takes in our body. We do not belong to ourselves but to Him. The resurrection life begins to reach us even at our point of weakness. We read,

Romans 8:11 "But if the Spirit of Him that raised Jesus from the dead dwells in you, He who raised Christ from the dead will also give life to your mortal bodies through His Spirit who dwells in you."

This is the next level we get to. We Christians are the only people who have the right to plead the blood of Jesus Christ over every ugly situation in our lives. There is power in the blood. When I see the blood, I will pass over you, says the Lord in the book of Exodus.

There is no amount of contamination that the blood of Jesus Christ cannot heal. He is the ultimate sacrifice, and there is power, wonder-working power, in the blood of Jesus Christ. He is the same yesterday today and forever. We believe that by calling on His name, trusting the finished work of Calvary, we can take hold of every challenge that comes by day and every terror that comes by night. God does not want us to be afraid of the terrors of the night (dreams). These things seem to be aggravated by night and darkness, and hence we hate them. We cannot see their approach, we cannot measure their outlines, and we know not the extent of the danger or what may be the calamity.

The devil realises he can get us at a point when we are weak. It's my encouragement to lay the foundation of God's word to start our day and declare His word as we lie down to sleep. God loves us, and He promised never to leave us nor forsake us Hebrews 13:5. We need to recognise the power given to us when we call on the name of Jesus Christ and know the power in His blood.

## Chapter 14

# DEMONIC DREAMS AND CONTAMINATION

1 Thessalonians 5:23:

> "Now may the God of peace Himself, sanctify you completely; and may your whole spirit, soul, and body be preserved at the coming of our Lord Jesus Christ."

> May you be kept in soul, mind and body in spotless integrity until the coming of our Lord. We should pray for complete holiness till we are presented faultless before the throne of His glory. God holds us responsible for what we do to our body, what we put in our soul—the mind and our feelings and the spirit.

We feed our spirit by staying in tune with the Holy Spirit; this may be done by our prayer life—constant communion with God. Our soul is fed by the word of

God, and listening to sound teaching keeps our soul in tune with God. When it comes to our body, we have a responsibility to keep our body clean, keep warm, eat well, and rest. This mandate to look after ourselves is a twenty-four/seven responsibility; this also means that we are responsible for what happens to us even in our sleep.

We cannot say we do not know what takes place the moment we go to bed because God has given us the responsibility to be alert and watch even as we rest in our beds. The night is a time of demonic activity, so we need to yield our body, soul, and spirit to the Lord to guard ourselves against contamination. The devil's war is to win souls, and he does not rest but is very active at night, taking control of men and women as they lie in bed. We can stop him by prayer and total surrender to the Lord.

**Incubus**

A legendary demon, an incubus is a *lilin*—demon in male form, which, according to mythological and legendary traditions, lies upon sleeping women to engage in sexual activity with them. Salacious tales of incubi (many demons) have been told for many centuries, and traditions hold that repeated sexual activity with an incubus may result in the deterioration of health, insanity, or even death. The word incubus is derived from late-Latin *incubo* (a nightmare induced by such a demon) from incubi i.e. (to lie upon). One of the earliest mentions of an incubus comes from Mesopotamia. In 2400 BC, the hero Gilgamesh's father, Lilu, disturbed and seduced women in their sleep. Other *lili*, called *ardat*, visit women and beget children by them. These demons were originally storm demons, but they eventually became regarded as night demons. (The above is paraphrased from the entry on Wikipedia)

## Succubus

Succubus is a demonic entity that appears to men in dreams and forces them to have sexual intercourse with men. This demon uses force, making it difficult for a man to get rid of it until it's done. When the man wakes up in the morning, he feels exhausted. He might even produce semen, and this is referred to as wet dreams. These men experience real pleasure as if in a real sexual encounter. These experiences, if not dealt with, can become repeated encounters. First, you need to understand why the spirits are attracted to certain people despite an absence of love. They always come when we have opened a door for them.

Christians are supposed to build a strong spiritual relationship with God, studying the word of God, praying in the Spirit, walking in submission to authority, and learning from God and from one another. Therefore, when Spiritual laws are broken, we find ourselves in a bad place where the demonic witch knows and understands Spiritual laws and begins to interfere in our lives. I have had some people come to me for prayer after mental torment from these demonic spirits. One man called this Spirit his wife. He believed his dead wife was coming back to have sex with him every night. He became so obsessed with these nocturnal encounters that it began to affect his work; he could not concentrate and could not form healthy relationships with females.

We know that this cannot be correct because the Bible says in Ecclesiastes 9:5–6:

> "5 For the living know that they will die;
> But the dead know nothing,
> And they have no more reward,
> For the memory of them is forgotten.
> 6 Also their love, their hatred, and their envy have now perished;
> Nevermore will they have a share
> In anything done under the sun."

Therefore, we need to get rid of all careless habits, including, watching pornography, watching horror movies, having multiple sexual partners, engaging in extramarital affairs, fornication, adultery, paedophilia, same-sex encounters, sexual abuse, molestation, rape, playing with sex toys, unnatural sexual habits sodomy bestiality (sleeping with animals). The Bible in Genesis 6:1-5 explains how spiritual beings came to have sexual encounters with human beings. The consequences of these demonic encounters will cause marriages to break down, miscarriages, and infertility. It affects mental health, finances, and relationships.

To deal with these, one has to develop a deeper relationship with God, repeating and reciting scriptures, build an altar in your home, have set times of prayer in the morning, noon, and night. Even if its ten minutes at a time, get into the habit of waking up early praying and reading the word. Surround yourself with prayerful people who can pray with you. Have set times to fast and desire an infilling of the Holy Spirit. If you are praying, use the name of Jesus Christ when you pray. You can start with repentance on behalf of yourself and your family. Keep a dream diary where you keep a record of your dreams of what is happening as you are praying. Most of these things are not spoken of in Church. Psychologists and health professionals also will attribute this to mental health issues, yet these things are real and in our society. One should not stop seeking help if confronted with these spirits.

Isaiah 34:11–15:

"But the pelican and the porcupine shall possess it,
Also the owl and the raven shall dwell in it.
And He shall stretch out over it
The line of confusion and the stones of emptiness.
They shall call its nobles to the kingdom,
But none *shall be* there, and all its princes shall be nothing.
And thorns shall come up in its palaces,
Nettles and brambles in its fortresses;
It shall be a habitation of jackals,
A courtyard for ostriches.
The wild beasts of the desert shall also meet with the jackals,
And the wild goat shall bleat to its companion;
Also the night creature shall rest there,
And find for herself a place of rest.

There the arrow snake shall make her nest and lay
*eggs*
And hatch, and gather *them* under her shadow;
There also shall the hawks be gathered,
Every one with her mate"
It describes demonic spirits that bring fear and
cause terror by night.

Chapter 15

# HUMAN SPIRITS

Apart from demonic spirits that come at night, there are also human spirits, working through witchcraft, and Asiates demons of astral projection, who visit people in their sleep to attack them. These things are propelled through lust. Pornography, impurity, romantic novels, and anything else that we open our minds to defile us, opens us to these attacks. Demons know what we like. They know what we spend our time on. The Bible says in

> (Leviticus 11:44,45; 19:2 and 1 Peter1:16) "Be holy as I am Holy."

By watching these things, we open ourselves up to demonic forces, and we invite them.

Human spirits and demonic spirits come to defile us. Jesus Christ came to make us pure, so as to serve God with purity, but the devil came to defile us and contaminate us. It is our duty as Christians to cry out to God in the name of Jesus Christ.

Isaiah 26:13 says, "O Lord our God, masters besides You Have had dominion6 over us; *But* by You only we make mention of Your name."

We can repeatedly call on the blood of Jesus Christ to wash us, to help us. Some people have found it easier to leave the light on at night to avoid attacks from these demons. Disobedience also opens these doors, giving him legal ground. Look for these doors and shut them. In summary, I've mentioned a few doors we open. Fornication, incest, adultery, homosexuality, sexual perversion, masturbation, pornography, unforgiveness, bitterness, carnality, worldliness, fear, doubt, laziness, witchcraft, rebellion and disobedience to parents and to authority, astrology, superstitions, chain letters, freemasonry, yoga, molestation, abuse, rape, soul ties, spirituality, engaging in unguided unnecessary spiritual warfare, religious witchcraft, throwing arrows at other people, always praying for people to die (witchcraft prayers), and ignorance of God's word. In all these, if we align ourselves to the Word of God and call on the Blood of Jesus Christ, we will have victory over these demonic spirits.

## Scientific Explanations on These Nightmares

In the field of medicine, here is what scientists have discovered. They describe "victims" who may have been experiencing waking dreams or sleep paralysis. The phenomenon of sleep paralysis is well established. During the first phase of sleep (also known as REM sleep), motor centres in the brain are inhibited, producing paralysis. The reason for this is ultimately unknown, but the most common explanation is that it prevents one from acting out one's dreams. Malfunctions of this process can result in either somnambulism (sleepwalking) or, conversely, sleep paralysis, where one remains partially or wholly paralysed for a short time after waking.

In some dreams, people feel being crushed or suffocated, electric tingles or vibrations, the imagined presence of a visible or invisible entity, and sometimes intense emotions of fear or euphoria and orgasmic feelings. These often appear quite real and vivid and could easily cause people to believe that a demon was holding them down. Nocturnal arousal could be explained by creatures causing otherwise guilt-producing behaviour. Add to this the common phenomena of nocturnal emission and all the elements required to believe in an incubus are present.

**What the Bible Says**

Genesis 6:1 says, "Now it came to pass, when men began to multiply on the face of the earth, and daughters were born to them, that the sons of God saw that the daughters of men were beautiful; and they took wives for themselves of all whom they chose."

Demon spirits were having sex with human beings.

In the Garden of Eden, Satan, who is a spirit, took a form of a serpent and began to talk to Eve. Sometimes we read in the story of Lot that the Lord took human form to go down to Sodom. This is a sign that it is possible for spirits to take on human form. Today, many people report that they have sexual encounters at night, which doctors dismiss as hallucinations.

I had a discussion with a woman in my office one day. We were praying for her to get married. She pointed out that she was still a virgin at the age of fifty, but she had experienced beautiful sex. Wanting to know more, I asked what she meant by that, and she went on to tell me of sexual encounters almost every night with her fiancé, who had died twenty years earlier in a car crash. One thing the devil is good at is deception. This lady believed in her heart that the man coming to her every night was her dead fiancé.

Many people have had encounters with demon spirits that manifest themselves at night. These spirits are often violent and will attack you—beating, choking, and restraining you. They are abusive and act as rapists.

Another effect these spirits have on people is overwhelming sexual urges in the body; you will know you are being attacked by demons if the sexual urges are so strong that they take over your mind. People end up having stronger orgasms than usual. This is not normal, reader. Seek help if you find yourself in this place, in repeated sex dreams and getting robbed of sleep.

Genesis 6:4 says,

"There were giants on the earth in those days, and also afterward, when the sons of God came in to the daughters of men and they bore children to them. Those were the mighty men who were of old, men of renown."

Married women who experience these encounters will stop having a normal relationship with their husbands. They are usually left emotionally and spiritually drained.

What they experience becomes more intense than normal sex. For young boys and girls, they become addicted to pornography and masturbation and become twisted. These spirits of sexual lust come to destroy and lead to many addictions. Remember, the battle is for your soul. Once the devil takes hold of your soul, it becomes very hard to walk in faith and grow in a loving relationship with the Lord.

If you find yourself caught up in all this, there is a way out. In the first place, disobedience to God's law opens the door to the enemy. Make sure you go to God in repentance of every known and unknown act of disobedience. Ask the Lord Jesus Christ to wash your mind, body, and soul in His blood. Feed yourself with the word of God and declare victory over contamination. Sometimes we open the door to these demonic spirits through our own ungodly desires. The movies we love to watch, the songs we listen to, the company we keep, the jokes we entertain—sometimes all of it makes us too lazy to pray and study God's word.

My friend, if you think you are having fun and enjoying the intense sexual ecstasy of demon spirits, remember, you will pay a high price for losing your soul to hell. You need to cut yourself off from these demons by crying out to God to help you. Remember, the devil does not give free gifts. That pleasure he gives has a price tag to it. That price tag is the destruction of your soul. He is in the business of contaminating souls so they become abominable to their Holy God. Whenever you have sex with these demon spirits, they leave you pregnant with lust, fear, rebellion, pornography, and all sorts of magic arts. These spirits affect you as a whole; they affect your health, your marriage, even your finances. I had a woman come to me and told me she was a widow for a long time and would not consider marriage because of the bond between her and her late husband. She explained to me that her husband comes to her at least once a week to make love to her. I warned her that this was a deception from the enemy.

> "For the living, know that they will die;
> But the dead know nothing,
> And they have no more reward,
> For the memory of them is forgotten.
> Also their love, their hatred, and their envy have now perished
> Nevermore will they have a share
> In anything done under the sun" (Ecclesiastes 9:5–6).

*Chapter 16*

# A DIVINE REVELATION

In 2015, I fell ill. I knew that I could die anytime. I asked God to spare me and allow me to raise my son, who at that time was thirteen years old. I always had a fear that if I died he would be left alone, and I worried a lot about him. I have other grown children whom I know have built a good relationship with the Lord and are able to go through life without me, but this young man needs a lot of guidance and direction, as I feel there is a calling of God in his life. He is a good child who tries to stay out of trouble, but spiritually he has not opened his heart to the Lord. These were the thoughts I kept having when I was unwell. I struggled with low iron in my blood, and the situation seemed to get worse.

One day, as I lay down in the lounge, which had become my sanctuary—I would stay most days and nights sleeping on the sofa or on the floor, praying most of the time—I felt my life ebbing away. I would get up and tidy the house, cook meals, and keep a happy face, yet inside I had this knowing that days were numbered. I attend a local prayer group where we meet every Thursday morning. Those days of my illness, we met at St Michaels, a Church of England in Sittingbourne. We pray for the nation, we pray for our country and its leadership, we pray for the church in Sittingbourne, and we pray for the body of Christ at large. We are a small group of just about ten members, and our leader, Ken Lurkhurst, is a faithful man of God who has had this prayer group for more then twenty years. God bless Ken. He is well known in the town as a godly and humble man.

One day, when I was unwell, a lady came to help me with housework. She prayed with me and went downstairs to clean and prepare food. I was alone in the lounge. I felt very weak and started to drift off into a deep sleep. I was aware of the little boy sitting in the lounge watching TV. He too fell asleep.

While I slept, I had a divine revelation. I felt I was in a dream and walking into what looked like a great white auditorium. This place was very white. The walls of this room looked *alive*—silky waterfalls, very difficult to describe. They looked magnificent beyond what human words can describe. As I walked into this room, I began to feel that I was the only person walking there. There was complete silence; all I could hear was the beating of my heart. I was aware of beings in this room and everything deathly quiet. I started to feel as if I was the object of judgement and speculation. I thought the eyes of all the beings in this place where on me.

I began to look at the order of this room. It looked like a courtroom, and I saw what looked like judges sitting in a row, which I call the first row. These beings were quiet, and they had open books in front of them. They were serious and did not look to the right or to the left. They concentrated on what they were doing. They were writing, and they did not raise their eyes to look at me. I sensed that they all had their eyes on me. I was terrified as I walked towards them. The silence and the seriousness of what was in front of me terrified me. I wondered what they were writing in those books. I asked what they were writing. This question came from within me, without moving my mouth or speaking with a voice out loud. Then I got an answer from these beings. They did not open their mouths, but I could clearly hear them say, "This is a record of all the works of men on the earth."

Revelation 20–12: "And I saw the dead, small and great, standing before God, and the books were opened. And another book was opened, which is the Book of Life. And the dead were judged according to their works, by the things which were written in the books."

When I stood in that place, I realised that a time will come upon all humanity that every man would stand as individual before God. Wealth, power, and fame will all be immaterial. For all children of God who have walked in uprightness and fear of God, it will be an ultimate blessing to stand before one who will give them eternal rewards.

I stood there looking and knowing that books recorded the good and bad deeds of those who live on earth. The record of all our works is in there before death.

I looked at these beings and saw some books open, and the beings were more magnificent in nature, and the books were a bit different. I wondered what they were writing. They were steadfast in what they were doing. They did not raise up their faces to look at me but continued to write. I wondered what they were writing, so I asked. They did not look at me but continued to write, but I could hear them speak. They were recording all the good deeds done by Christians on earth.

Revelation 22:12: "And behold, I am coming quickly, and My reward is with me, to give to every one according to his work."

Revelation 3:21: "To Him who overcomes I will grant to sit with Me on My throne, as I also overcame and sat down with My Father on His throne."

God is setting up His eternal Kingdom. He uses trials and tests while we are on this earth, but a day is coming where every good deed we have done, publically or in secret, will be recognised and rewarded. No work is lost as everything is recorded. I stood there, and all I could hear was the thudding of my heart, which was at that point the only noise in that place.

I then looked up and saw some more magnificent tall beings. These were not sitting but standing. They held trumpets and were standing poised as if they were about to blow their trumpets. I was made aware of the sound, which seemed to be a clock going *tick tick tick tick*. This sound made me aware of time. I realised that these majestic beings holding trumpets were awaiting instruction, at the sound or tick of a certain, the clock is counting down to the last day. At that realisation, I became terrified.

I looked onto my side and saw one who looked looked more beautiful than words can describe. He had a book and was writing. As I looked at this book, I knew without anyone telling me that it was the Book of Life. I started to walk towards the one who has power over life and death. I walked towards Him and began to ask.

In my thoughts, I knew that if the clock hit a certain note, the ones with the trumpets would blow them and everything on earth would stop, and man would have reached the final destiny either to be rewarded or condemned according to what was written in the books. I was terrified. I began to question my own walk with the Lord. Have I lived my life in obedience to His call? I was fearful. I asked, "Is my name written in that book?"

His face still looking in the book, and yet, feeling His intense look into my eyes.

"What is the day today?" He asked.

"Thursday," I answered.

"What are you supposed to do on a Thursday?"

"I go to the prayer group"

"Why are you not there?"

"I am not well. Can't you see I am unwell?"

"Is that how you behave when you are not well and supposed to be at work?"

I realised this was a serious matter. My thoughts went back to my work in the NHS. When I'm running late, I call them to let them know I will be late for work. When I am sick, I let them know I can't come to work, and this is so I can keep my job. This respect and honour I give to the NHS is because I know they pay me at the end of the month so I can pay my bills. My attitude to the things of God should be better.

I struggled while I stood there. My excuse was not good enough. Then I began to think, *What is this small prayer group that I attend with few people? It's not even my church. I just joined them. Why must such a small thing condemn me?* The Lord reminded me I had not just chosen to be part of that prayer group, but He had called me there. I began to ask the Lord to forgive me and please give me another chance.

My favourite scripture is:-

2 Corinthians 5:10–11: "For we must all appear before the judgement seat of Christ, that each one may receive the things done in the body, according to what he has done, whether good or bad. Knowing therefore, the terror of the Lord, we persuade men; but we are well known to God, and I also trust are well known in your consciences."

# PART 2

## Chapter 17

# DREAM SYMBOLS

This short section describes dreams and some common symbols and meanings of some common colours. This writing is not a prescription on what the symbols mean.

Numbers 12:6:
"Then He said,
Hear now My words:
If there is a prophet among you,
I, the Lord, make Myself known to him in a vision;
I speak to him in a dream."

We have established in this writing that God desires to speak to His people all the time, but because we have not developed a stable relationship, we have not wanted to hear His voice. We have not trained our spirit to decode spiritual messages because our day is busy and we cannot be still. The Lord finds a way to communicate to us. We have also established that dreams are a language of the Holy Spirit and should not be ignored but great consideration needs to be made to establish what God is saying to us.

Everyone should develop their own dream language, as this differs from culture to culture. However, there are common symbols that seem to almost mean the same things across cultures. Many Christians will agree with most symbols that mean the same thing across cultures. The list is not exclusive but will attempt as much as possible to list most common symbols.

## Colours

White:
Purity; holiness; Robe of Righteousness; pursuing Christ; God's lightening power; awakening; virginity; Hosts of Heaven; wedding; marriage; priesthood; harvest; victory; blessings; joy; angels; peace; triumph.

Black:
Ephraim's son and Manasseh's tribal stone, also called onyx—a result of fire or burning; burning away the flesh taking on the nature of Christ; the clouds covering the presence of God;

Psalm 18:11. "He made darkness His secret place;
His canopy around Him was dark waters
And thick clouds of the skies."

Death and destruction, mourning, God changing bad situations, God hides His treasures in dark places; we need to search them out, darkness, broaching, darkness, sin.

Blue:
Wisdom; truth; heaven; eternity; devotion; peace; loyalty; openness; healing; justice; peace with self and others. Blue is peace to any storm in life.

**The presence of God.**

Navy Blue (Sapphire):
The colour under God's feet; wisdom; beauty of God's law (Exodus 24:10, Ezekiel 10:1). Tribe of Dan Naphtali and Asher. Jesus Christ wears blue on His belt. Blue speaks of royalty. Blue is for kings, and God has called us to rule on this earth.

Maroon or Dark Red:
Wine; covenant relationship with the Father through Jesus Christ; overcoming, victory; communion with God.

Red:
The blood of Jesus Christ; forgiveness of sin; healing; deliverance; salvation; Fire of the Holy Spirit; mercy and sacrifice; maturity in Christ; sin of man; brings life to our bodies.

Pink:
Mixture of red and white; revival; new birth; priesthood; innocence in childhood; childlike heart; gentleness; kindness.

Fuchsia (Dark Pink):
Passion; deep passion for God; joy (Psalm 149:3); intercession; conception of Godly ideas.

Purple (Royalty or Priesthood):
King of Kings; unity; royalty; authority; discernment; heavenly provision; impartation in ministry; ambassadors of the kingdom; intercessors; portals of heaven; a gift to download from heaven; touching heaven and changing earth; God's justice.

Yellow/Gold:
Oil in the lamps in the temple; our inheritance; His presence; anointing; glory; He gives us the oil of gladness and to keep us burning with a love and passion for Him; yield/grace to yield; associated with fire—purification.

Orange:
The prophetic anointing; listening to and hearing/seeing what God is saying or doing and being able to connect with Him in the Spirit. Lamps produced on orange flame; priestly calling; power; speaks loudly of God's might and ability. Fire of God/passionate praise.

Brown:
Servant-hood, humility; the colour of Jesus Christ's clothes on earth (the shepherds wore brown); the shepherd's rod

was brown; the sling and stones used by David to kill the giant were brown; unless a seed falls to the ground (brown seed—brown ground) and dies it abides alone; Jesus Christ, the bread of life (brown is the colour of service and humility); end of a season; weariness; faint.

Green:
The Word of God; immortality; the leaf shall not wither Psalms 1:3; resurrection; new life; spring—a new season; praise; growth; prosperity; restoration.

Turquoise:
River of God; sanctification; healing; New Jerusalem.

Silver:
The Word of God; purity; divinity; salvation; truth; atonement; redemption.

## Symbols

Book
- The purpose of a book is to preserve information.
- (Psalm 56:8) "You number my wanderings;
  Put my tear into Your bottle;
  Are they not in Your? book."
- An audit of one's life
  (Revelation 20:12),
  "And I saw the dead, small and great, standing before God, and the books were opened. And another book was opened, which is the Book of Life. And the dead were judged according to their

works, by the things which were written in the
books."

The dead were judged according to what was
written.

- All the sins that don't appear obvious are recorded.
(Psalm 40:7)
"Then I said, "Behold, I come;
In the scroll of the book it is written about me."

- Psalm 139:14–16.
"I will praise You, for I am fearfully and
wonderfully made;
Marvelous are Your works,
And that my soul knows very well.
My frame was not hidden from You,
When I was made in secret,
And skillfully wrought in the lowest parts of the
earth.
Your eyes saw my substance, being yet unformed.
And in Your book they all were written.
The days fashioned for me,
When as yet there were none of them."

- Psalm 69:28.
"Let them be blotted out of the book of the living,
And not be written with the righteous."

- Book of Life
(Philippians 4:3)
"And I urge you also, true companion, help these
women who laboured with me in the gospel, with
Clement also, and the rest of my fellow workers,
whose names are in the Book of Life"

Revelation 3:5.

"He who overcomes shall be clothed in whit garments, and I will not blot out his name from te Book of Life, but I will confess his name before my Father and before His angels."

- The Book of Life has the names of the citizens of Heaven.
- Books will be opened.
- Book could mean instruction to read the word of God.

(Ezekiel 3:3)

"And He said to me, "Son of man, feed your belly, and fill your stomach with this scroll that I give you." So I ate, and it was in my mouth like honey in sweetness."

Eat the scroll acquaint yourself with the word of God.

Baby

- If you see you are holding or given a baby, this means you are about to nurture and feed. It could mean a young ministry and responsibility to take care of it.
- A sick or skinny baby could mean lack of nourishment. If you are a pastor, pray for wisdom to develop skills to feed the Church, and nurture it until it comes to maturity.
- Sometimes you are that baby in need of nourishment from the Father, where we draw spiritual milk of the word.

- We are vulnerable and need His guidance and protection at all times.
- Soiled baby. There is need to clean up. Repent/ start afresh.
- Need of attention.
- Love.

Tree

- Your life; the roots mean your foundation, background, history, spiritual history.
- The branches are your connections with other people in the past and present.
- (Size of tree) big great tree may symbolise growth and where God is taking you.
- Fruit (much fruit) means the potential to be productive in your life.
- Trunk (big) stability and balance.
- Being able to stand against pressure.
- Different kinds of fruit in one tree—diverse gifting/ministries in one person, there could be apostolic/prophetic gifting, evangelistic/healing ministries teaching/pastoral gifting help, all kinds of ministries of help.
- Tree can also mean being grounded and rooted. (Psalm 92:13)
  "Those who are planted in the house of the Lord, Shall flourish in the courts of our God."

Climbing a tree

- Lifting up
- Attaining new levels, a higher place

- Cutting down a tree
- Pursuing goals that waste your time/foolishness
- A waste of time

Falling tree
- Disgrace/walking on the wrong path pursuing the wrong goals.
  (Matthew 7:19)
  "Every tree that does not bear good fruit is cut down, and thrown into the fire".
  (Daniel 4:14)
  "He cried aloud and said thus
  "Chop down the tree and cut off its branches,
  Strip off its leaves and scatter its fruit.
  Let the beasts get out from under it.
  And the birds from its branches."

River—flowing
- Revival
- Moves of God
- Ice and snow represent spiritual things
- Blessings from God
- Swimming in dirty water can mean you need healing and have issues to be addressed

Naked
- To dream you are naked means you are going to be exposed
- Shamed
- It's a negative dream

Staircase
- Positive uplifting moments, going up the staircase, moving up towards your goal
- Attaining a spiritual goal
- Progress

Falling Down the Stairs
- Things are getting out of control—work, family, ministry project—these may be crumbling.

House
- Represents your life or spiritual state
  (Matthew 7:24–27
  "Therefore whoever hears these sayings of Mine, and does them, I will liken him to a wise man who built his house on the rock. And the rain descended, the floods came, and the winds blew and beat on that house; and it did not fall, for it was founded on the rock. But everyone who hears these sayings of Mine, and does not do them, will be like a foolish man who built his house on the sand: and the rain descended, the floods came, and the winds blew and beat on that house; and it fell. And great was its fall."
  2 Timothy 2:19
  "Nevertheless the solid foundation of God stands, having this seal: "The Lord knows those who are His," and, "Let everyone who names the name of Christ depart from iniquity.""
- New house—new area of ministry
- Leaking roof—lack of spiritual covering

- Broken roof—God's protection removed due to sin
- Filthy house—sin, presence of sin, wrong choices
- Many rooms—many gifts new openings, opportunities
- Castle—security/strong protection
- Dark house means bad memories that we don't want to talk about
- Clean, well lit—presence of the Holy Spirit
- Represents authority
- Moving house—going through a major life change
- Putting the past behind

Burning house
- End of relationship, if the fire is destructive, then something dear to you is about to be destroyed completely
- Sabotage on the way
- Something you are building is falling apart
- Two-storey/three-storey house indicates more responsibilities/talents/gifts or power given to you
- Greater calling and maturity, mentoring responsibilities over others

Warehouse
- Provisions of God in store for you
- God wants to give you more than you know or expect

Jail
- Bondage/limitation

Petrol station

- Driving to a petrol station means you need filling up. Stop what you are doing go to a place of seeking God; do not be alone; be around people who can encourage you
- A place for renewing—it could be church or conference where you get refreshing to keep you going or to get you to the next level
- A place of encouragement or empowering
- More grace/more power

Tent

- Temporary, must move on, not permanent
- Maybe instability or unstable
- David wanted to build a house for the Lord instead of a tent temporary structure

Table

- Sitting at a table means communion, people with the same agenda
- Positive God bringing likeminded people into your life
- A church fellowship, meeting up together for the purposes of Christ
  1 Corinthians 10:16
  "The cup of blessing which we bless, is it not the communion of the blood of Christ? The bread which we break, is it not the communion of the body of Christ?"

- If the room is dark and you are sitting at a table, it could also mean meeting up for ungodly demonic purposes

Keys

- Keys represent authority—to open up or to lock up
- One key means a responsibility
- Many keys—many opportunities and responsibilities
- Many ministries/giftings
- Rusty keys—missed opportunities/lost chances, neglected duties
- Not paying attention to a given opportunity, gift, or opening
- New key—new doors/opportunity, new mandate/ calling
- Found a new key—you have found solution to a problem/old problem
- Lost keys—lost opportunities, lost control over responsibilities
- Stolen keys—losing your opportunities, power to someone, someone taking your place or you share a vision with someone and they go ahead and do what you are meant to do
- A bunch of keys—ability to serve in many positions (pastor, mother, wife, counsellor), more knowledge
- A gold key—more influential role, power, wealth

Aeroplane

- Ministry—mission a work that will touch nations a great ministry
- Powerful dynamic work
- A great anointing to soar higher than average
- An ability to influence many people
- Diversity of giving
- Ability to influence and empower many generations and types of people
- Big plane stands for a large ministry or organisation to do with many people
- Small fighter jets may mean intercessory ministry, spiritual warfare, ministries dealing with great power to operate in the spiritual realm, high calling on evangelical ministry
- Air-force type—fighter aeroplanes with equipment, awareness of heavy spiritual battles, power to fight demonic powers, knowledge and insight into the spiritual realm, prophetic intercession
- Commercial aeroplanes/cargo—opening for business activities influencing different levels of people
- Flying too low is bad—very little prayer life
- Air crash—broken dreams, failure, being grounded, end of a vision, destruction; survivors—Church can be destroyed or left with only a few people

Vehicles

- In each of the symbols you see (the size and the movement), be diligent to discern the correct meaning. God is speaking to you the way He did to Pharaoh, Daniel, and Nebuchadnezzar. Ignoring dreams is very detrimental to Christian growth.

- Any vehicles indicate one has a calling in their lives. The size will determine where you are going; a big vehicle means a big ministry.
- If you are alone in a vehicle, this means managing your own relationship, moving from glory to glory. If with people, this means you have been given responsibility over other people. It could mean a family or small prayer group.
- If the vehicle has many people, you are responsible for taking a ministry (a Church) to its destination.
- If the vehicle is covered, this means spiritual cover; if open, this means spiritual exposure (this could mean sin is to be exposed)—not submitting to authority.
- If it breaks down, this might indicate mean challenges, difficulties, or sickness in the ministry.
- Puncture—temporary setback.
- Engine knocks or stops—hindrances.
- Crash—presence of sin, one's ministry getting ruined, lost souls, corruption disrupting movement, wrecked ministry.
- Car battery—being recharged.

I had a dream in 2016 in which I saw myself driving my car along a familiar A2 road. I saw the light on the car indicating my oil was running out. I needed to get on to a garage along the A2 to fill up before the car crashed. When I woke up, a friend called me asking if I was attending a conference at Robins Church, where a powerful anointed man of God, John Shiver from America, was speaking. I was unaware of this conference but decided to go. When I got there, the presence of the Lord was awesome. I had been feeling discouraged and down, almost ready to throw in the towel for all ministry work, but that conference brought me a new hope. I felt refreshed and understood the dream in full.

Bicycle
- Legalism, works of the flesh
- Self-righteousness
- Working out with one's strength, not relying on God

Ship/boat
- Church or ministry, powerful ministry progressing or being moved by the spirit of God
- Battleship—spiritual warfare

Bus
- Hebrews 11:9
  "By faith he dwelt in the land of promise as *in* a foreign country, dwelling in tents with Isaac and Jacob, the heirs with him of the same promise;"
- We are all on a journey on the same bus
- Ministry (if you are driving)
- A teaching ministry (if directing others)
- If a passenger then one of the others
- Unity in a body

Driving off a road
- Making load decisions
- Being irresponsible
- Putting other people's lives at risk
- Being out of control of your life
- Warning that you are being reckless

Lost/stolen car
- Loss of motivation, drive, interest in the ministry
- Lack of knowledge of how to get to the next level
- Uncertainty
- Running over people in your car—you have wounded people in the process of trying to achieve your goals
- You are involved in a car accident—you need to slow down before you hurt yourself and hurt others (you are being reckless in your life)

Train
- God uses the Church in the Spirit realm. Trains, unlike other modes of transportation, require a special track—take this into consideration. The bus and the motor car/cycle/bicycle all use roads, but a train has a special track meant for it.
- The train has compartment and classes. When I was growing up, the first class was for those who could afford to pay more. People could sleep on beds and eat a meal. The second class was comfortable, with beds, but six people had to share one car. The third class had a room in which a few people could sit and be comfortable, and the

fourth class had all sorts of people, sitting and standing, with no privacy.

- Our journey is the same to those who are willing to pay the price for righteousness and turn away from sin can be accommodated in the narrow way.

Matthew 7:13

"Enter by the narrow gate; for wide *is* the gate and broad *is* the way that leads to destruction, and there are many who go in by it."

The highway to hell is broad, and its gate is wide for the many who choose to pass through.

- The train announces t its coming. For His Church, there will be a trumpet call in the sky.
- The train has the capacity to carry goods and people.
- Derailed train—God may bring people together to function as an intercessory ministry, after which they start a Church and begin to face serious problems. If God shows you a derailed train he wants you to get back on track.
- A train has different parts, some meant to carry goods, some people.
- Five-fold ministry—one who drives a train has greater capacity to carry other ministries. Prophetic/apostolic/teacher/pastor/evangelist/ intercessor ministries of help. God's word and spirit can keep the train on track.
- Train as transport—one day I dreamt of a relative, a loved one, jumping onto a train, and a few days later this loved one died.

- The train as a bride of Christ—in these end times the Lord is preparing his people and the voice of the Arch angel will sound.

1 Thessalonians 4:15–16:

"For this we say to you by the word of the Lord, that we who are alive *and* remain until the coming of the Lord will by no means precede those who are [d]asleep. [16] For the Lord Himself will descend from heaven with a shout, with the voice of an archangel, and with the trumpet of God. And the dead in Christ will rise first."

- The train in your dream could be a warning to prepare for our final destination. We are called to watch and pray and always be ready when we hear that sound. We leave everything and jump on the eternal train. If you are ill and keep dreaming a train is coming, or if you miss the train, pray and make peace with God so that on the day the warning sounds, you are ready to jump on for a one-way trip. Reader, remember, everyone on this earth will get on that death train one day, even if the Lord tarries.

Daniel 12:2 warns,

"And many of those who sleep in the dust of the earth shall awake,

Some to everlasting life,

Some to shame *and* everlasting [a]contempt.

Recurrent train dreams indicate it may be the time to get serious with God and prepare to travel and meet with Him.

## Horses

- Many symbols of war
  Jeremiah 6:23,
  "They will lay hold on bow and spear;
  They *are* cruel and have no mercy;
  Their voice roars like the sea;
  And they ride on horses,
  As men of war set in array against you, O daughter of Zion."
  Deuteronomy 17:16.
  "But he shall not multiply horses for himself, nor cause the people to return to Egypt to multiply horses, for the Lord has said to you, 'You shall not return that way again.
- White horse—justice, holiness. Christ will return on a White Horse. It may mean death for a saint, joy, victory.
- Black horse—death of an ungodly person.
- Red horse—war, bloodshed, persecution, punishment
  Zachariah 1:8–11
  "I saw by night, and behold, a man riding on a red horse, and it stood among the myrtle trees in the hollow; and behind him *were* horses: red, sorrel, and white. [9] Then I said, "My lord, what *are* these?" So the angel who talked with me said to me, "I will show you what they *are*."

[10] And the man who stood among the myrtle trees answered and said, "These *are the ones* whom the Lord has sent to walk to and fro throughout the earth."

[11] So they answered the Angel of the Lord, who stood among the myrtle trees, and said, "We have walked to and fro throughout the earth, and behold, all the earth is [a]resting quietly."

- Horse—sin and lust
  Jeremiah 5:8
  "They were *like* well-fed lusty stallions; Every one neighed after his neighbor's wife., pride, wild and disorderly conduct, rebelliousness, impurity

  Psalm 32:9
  "Do not be like the horse *or* like the mule,
  *Which* have no understanding,
  Which must be harnessed with bit and bridle,
  Else they will not come near you.

  Jeremiah 8:6
  "I listened and heard,
  *But* they do not speak aright.
  No man repented of his wickedness,
  Saying, 'What have I done?'
  Everyone turned to his own course,
  As the horse rushes into the battle.

Donkey
- Servant animal, animal of burden, associated with humility, honour, stubbornness, endurance, loyalty.

• A man of God recently asked me to interpret a dream he had. He had seen a donkey and a big snake coming to attack the donkey. The donkey took the snake by the tail and began to tear it up. It went on to use its feet to crush its head. The meaning of that dream was that the pastor was that donkey and the Lord was equipping him to take the deception of the enemy until he had taken control of the whole situation. He ended up destroying the head, so the problem was going to be solved and the enemy completely defeated.

Snake

• Threat to your wellbeing, symbol of temptation, malicious enemy, betrayal, deception, trials, tests, someone trying to harm you, negativity, untrustworthiness, a warning to be careful some evil power, chaos from the underworld, divination, witchcraft, Satan/the devil

Revelation 12:9
"So the great dragon was cast out, that serpent of old, called the Devil and Satan, who deceives the whole world; he was cast to the earth, and his angels were cast out with him.
fabrication, demonic activity.

Dog

• Unclean animals. This is an animal that can have sex in front of its master; there is no shame in a dog. It eats unclean things, including its own vomit. Jesus, in

Mark 7:27 says,

"But Jesus said to her, "Let the children be filled first, for it is not good to take the children's bread and throw *it* to the little dogs.""

Dogs inside the Church represent sin and corruption, contamination, filthy desires.

Revelation 22:15:

"But outside *are* dogs and sorcerers and sexually immoral and murderers and idolaters, and whoever loves and practices a lie."

Outside are the dogs, sorcerers, whoremongers.

Deuteronomy 23:18:

"You shall not bring the wages of a harlot or the price of a dog to the house of the Lord your God for any vowed offering, for both of these *are* [g]an abomination to the Lord your God."

You shall not bring the price of a dog into the house of God for any vow. David says in

Psalm 22:16–20,

"He may dwell with you in your midst, in the place which he chooses within one of your gates, where it [b]seems best to him; you shall not oppress him.

[17] "There shall be no *ritual* [c]harlot of the daughters of Israel, or a perverted[d] one of the

sons of Israel. [18] You shall not bring the wages of a harlot or the price of a dog to the house of the Lord your God for any vowed offering, for both of these *are* [g]an abomination to the Lord your God.

[19] "You shall not charge interest to your brother—interest on money *or* food *or* anything that is lent out at interest. [20] To a foreigner you may charge interest, but to your brother you shall not charge interest, that the Lord your God may bless you in all to which you set your hand in the land which you are entering to possess.

Dogs have compassed me. Surrounded by enemies of God or evildoers, those who take the word of God lightly or have no regard for the truth, worthlessness, lack of self-control, anger and viciousness toward others. To dream of being bitten by a dog means people will attack you. To dream a dog on a leaf is self-control, tearing a dog apart. Fighting a dog means taking charge over a situation, overcoming a bad habit.

Fish

- Many fish—a great harvest of souls. Many years ago, preaching in a small town, I dreamt I caught a lot of small fish. It turned out many young people, of school-going age, came to the Lord. For some people it may mean money coming your way. Catching a big fish means a breakthrough, a big achievement.
- Catching a dead fish—to experience some loss, disappointment, being let down, death of a

friendship, relationship, losing members from the ministry.

Lion

- This can either be positive or negative; it may mean the Lord Jesus or His counterfeit (the devil).
- One day I dreamt I was in a thick forest. As I walked, there was a lion walking on my side. I was fearful of the many lions in the forest. The lion walking with me told me not to fear, as all the other lions were "pretend" lions. I must watch as they opened their mouths to roar. I noticed they all didn't have teeth. I was laughing and remembered

  1 Peter 5:8

  "Be [c]sober, be [d]vigilant; [e]because your adversary the devil walks about like a roaring lion, seeking whom he may devour."—Be sober and vigilant because your adversary, the devil, prowls around like a roaring lion. (But, in reality, he is not).
- Great strength, courage, aggression and power, king, dignity, royalty, leadership, pride, and dominion, your need to control others.

Monkey

- Deceit, immaturity, playful nature, mischief, hypocrisy, sabotage, disorganised, demonic presence.

Money
- Picking coins—in some cultures, this is a bad dream, yet money is always gain, picking up what is lost, increased responsibility and achievement, having a lot more value than before, acquiring value and grace
- Gold coins—valuable resources coming your ways. Priceless networks, picking up partnerships, friends, or helpers in the ministry.
- Losing coins—losing out on opportunities, valuable people leaving you, someone stealing from you or someone taking credit for your hard work.

Bulls
- Charging bull—demonic attacks, a lot of pressure Psalm 22:12

    "Many bulls have surrounded Me; Strong *bulls* of Bashan have encircled Me. Suffering ahead. Men/furious people showing aggression towards you.

Ox
- Service without aggression, strength, patient effort, self-sacrifice, willingness to serve under authority

Crossroads
- A point of making a decision, parting ways

Road
- Calling to follow a certain path

Mountains
- Desire to achieve, challenges
- Climbing—getting towards a desired goal or ambition, reaching to the top, ambition, prosperity/favour of God
- Moving mountains—faith in God
  Psalm 12:1
  "Help,[b] Lord, for the godly man ceases!
  For the faithful disappear from among the sons of men.

Mud
- Walking in mud—sin or muddy water means wrong doctrine

Police/soldiers
- Demonic presence

Broom
- Need to clean up an area in your life

**Some Dream Meanings**

- Naked—to be shamed or exposed
- Staircase—upward, positive, uplifting moments coming
- Downwards—failure
- Water—blessing
- Fire—cleansing, purifying, testing
- Birds—dove peace, joy
- Castle—house, security

- Lion—the Lord Jesus's protection
- Dog—sin, adultery, fornication
- Smoking—pride, rebellion
- Rain—blessings
- Keys—authority, many keys = different openings, higher authority, a positive opportunity coming up
- Rusty keys—missed opportunity
- Water rain spiritual river, blessing light rain blessings
- Vehicle—moving ministry moving from one level to another (a good dream)
- Abandoned car unused or abandoned vision/ministry
- Abortion—death or premature death of a ministry or vision
- Snake—spiritual enemies or deception
- Adultery—path of destruction
  Proverbs 2:16
  "To deliver you from the immoral woman, From the seductress *who* flatters with her words,"

- Sex—having sex is not from God see (Incubus/Succubus)
- Aeroplane—worldwide ministry or promotion
- Airport/ bus stop—departure could mean death moving to the next life or moving from one life to another
- Drinking alcohol—addiction (not good)
- Flowers peaches/mangoes or any fruit tree/flowers—sign of great potential or anointing upon a ministry

- Snakes—demonic spirits
  Isaiah 59:4–5
  "No one calls for justice,
  Nor does *any* plead for truth.
  They trust in empty words and speak lies;
  They conceive [b]evil and bring forth iniquity.
  [5] They hatch vipers' eggs and weave the spider's web;
  He who eats of their eggs dies,
  And *from* that which is crushed a viper breaks out."

- Angels—God's helpers and a sign of protection
  Hebrews 1:14
  "Are they not all ministering spirits sent forth to minister for those who will inherit salvation?"
- Animals—demonic spirits
- Telephone—receiving a message from God
- Antenna—need to pay attention to God (listen to God)

# About The Book

Should we attach any importance to our dreams? Can we teach ourselves to dream? We dream almost every night, but we often fail to grasp the importance of the message being downloaded to us from the spiritual realm.

Dreams carry personal messages to us and offer us opportunities to better understand our lives to achieve greater inner harmony. Dreams help us to solve practical personal problems and show us a way forward in times of trials and persecutions. We should seek to understand dreams and ask the Lord for the meaning of each dream, aligning them to the Word of God.